Air Fryer Cookbook

1500 Days of Quick & Easy Recipes to Make Delicious Homemade Meals with Less Effort | Bonus: Time Saving Hacks for Busy People & Much More

Linda Roberts

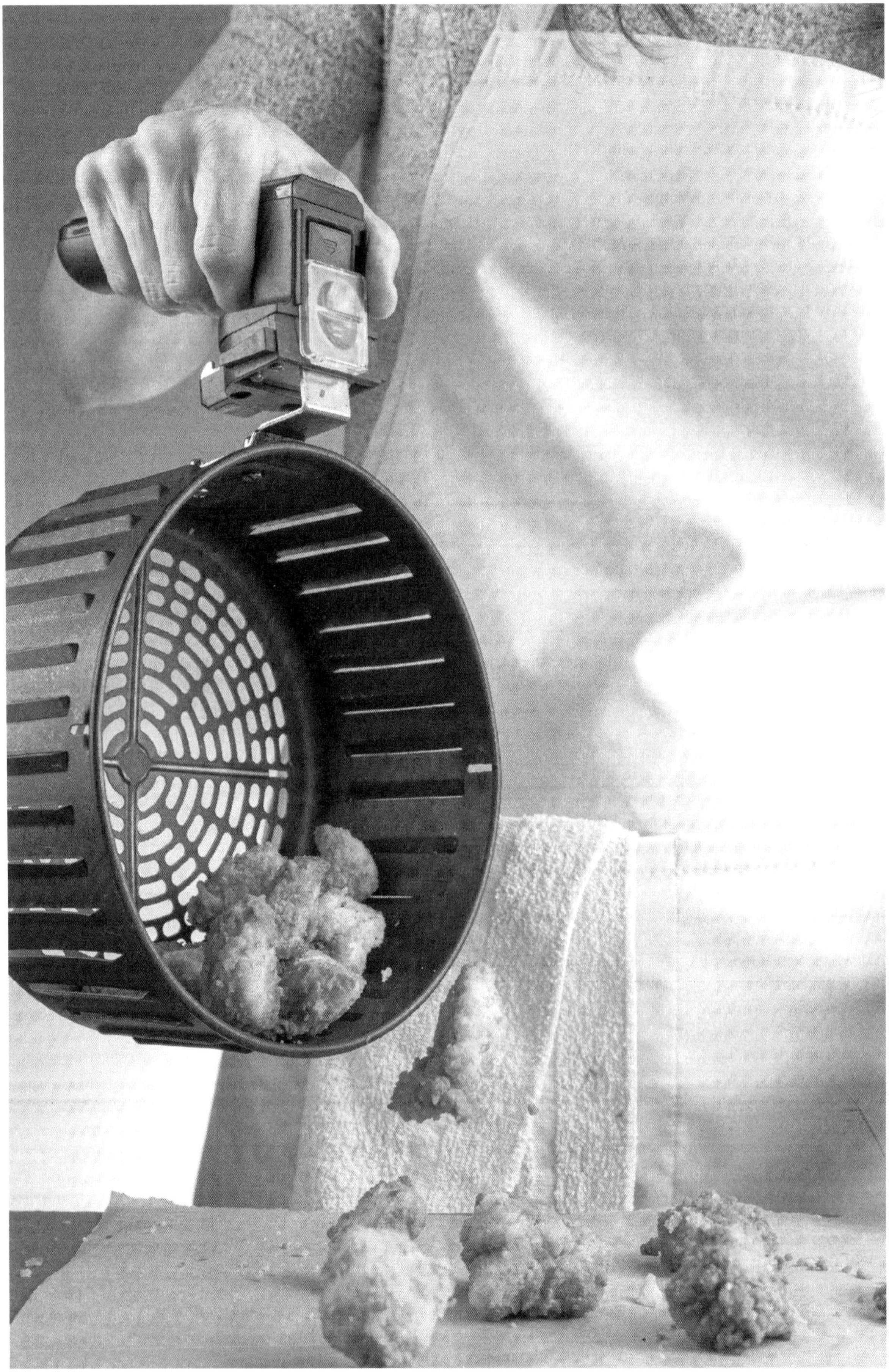

© **Copyright 2022 by Linda Roberts All rights reserved.**

This document is geared towards providing exact and reliable information regarding the topic and issue covered. The publication is sold with the idea that the publisher is not required to render accounting, officially permitted, or otherwise qualified services. If advice is necessary, legal or professional, a practiced individual in the profession should be ordered.

From a Declaration of Principles which was accepted and approved equally by a Committee of the American Bar Association and a Committee of Publishers and Associations.

In no way is it legal to reproduce, duplicate, or transmit any part of this document in either electronic means or in printed format. Recording of this publication is strictly prohibited and any storage of this document is not allowed unless with written permission from the publisher. All rights reserved.

The information provided herein is stated to be truthful and consistent, in that any liability, in terms of inattention or otherwise, by any usage or abuse of any policies, processes, or Instructions contained within is the solitary and utter responsibility of the recipient reader. Under no circumstances will any legal responsibility or blame be held against the publisher for any reparation, damages, or monetary loss due to the information herein, either directly or indirectly.

Respective authors own all copyrights not held by the publisher.

The information herein is offered for informational purposes solely and is universal as so. The presentation of the information is without contract or any type of guaranteed assurance.

The trademarks that are used are without any consent and the publication of the trademark is without permission or backing by the trademark owner. All trademarks and brands within this book are for clarifying purposes only and are owned by the owners themselves, not affiliated with this document.

Table of Contents:

Introduction 8

Chapter 1: Step-By-Step Air Frying 10

Chapter 2: Time Saving Hacks 15

Chapter 3: A Week Of Meal Prep 16

Chapter 4: Breakfast Recipes 19

Fluffy Breakfast Donuts 19

Air Fried Grit Patties Breakfast 19

Breakfast Egg Muffins 20

French Toast With Blueberries 20

Egg Rolls 21

Whole Meal Cinnamon Toast 21

Granola Breakfast 22

Air Fried Mushroom Frittata 22

Air Fried Pecan Oat Breakfast 23

Breakfast Hash browns 23

Sausage Breakfast 24

Flat Breakfast Bread 24

Eggs In Avocado 25

Whole Wheat Banana Toast 25

Air Fried Pancakes 26

Cloud Pancakes 26

Chapter 5: Snack And Appetizers Recipes 27

Air Fried Brussels Sprouts 27

Air Fried Eggplants With Zaatar 27

Air Fried Potato Skins 28

Crispy Feta Cheese Fries 28

Broccoli Fritters 29

Air Fried Mushrooms 29

Air Fried Potatoes 29

Air Fried Broccoli Florets With Sesame Seeds 30

Air Fried Avocado 30

Potato Chips 31

Stuffed Avocado 31

Stuffed Mushrooms 31

Air Fried Onion 32

Air Fried Cheese Sticks 32

Air Fried Asparagus 33

Air Fried Radish 33

Air Fried Green Beans 34

Air Fried Apple Chips 34

Wrapped Halloumi Cheese With Bacon 34

Kale Chips 35

Air Fried Tomatoes 35

Chapter 6: Vegetables And Sides 36

Air Fried Vegetables 36

Air Fried Potato Bake 36

Jalapeno Wraps With Bacon 37

Breadsticks 37

Air Fried Carrots 38

Air Fried Acorn Squash 38

Air Fried Pizza 38

Asian-Style Vegetable Spring Rolls 39

Air Fried Chickpeas 39

Air Fried Potato Buns 39

Air Fried Potato Fritters 40

Air Fried Potatoes And Beets 40

Air Fried Mushrooms With Teriyaki Sauce ... 40

Air Fried Cashews With Paprika 41

Air Fried Farro Salad 41

Air Fried Crispy Tofu With Cornstarch Salad 42

Tofu And Lettuce Salad 42

Air Fried Bell Pepper Salad 43

Air Fried Vegetables Salad 43

Air Fried Beet And Carrots Veggie Salad 43

Air Fried Bacon And Sweet Potato Salad 44

Air Fried Aspragus Salad 44

Air Fried Egg And Avocado Salad 45

Air Fried Pear Salad 45

Air Fried Bacon And Sweet Potato Salad 46

Air Fried Potatoes And Parsnips Salad 46

Air Fried Caesar Salad 47

Chapter 7: Poultry Mains Recipes 48

Air Fried Chicken Breasts 48

Air Fried Turkey Tenders 48

Air Fried Tandoori Chicken 48

Air Fried Cheese Chicken Wings 49

Chicken Nuggets With Mayonnaise 49

Burrito Chicken 50

Air Fried Paprika Chicken 50

Air Fried Cheddar Chicken Muffins 51

Air Fried Whole Chicken 51

Air Fried Chicken Chops With Cashews 51

Air Fried Chicken With Broccoli 52

Air Fried Buffalo Chicken With Blue Cheese . 52

Air Fried Chicken Bites 53

Chicken Spinach Nest 53

Air Fried Chicken Thighs 54

Air Fried Chicken Wings 54

Air Fried Chinese Style Chicken 55

Air Fried Stuffed Chicken 55

Chicken Stuffed Macaroni With Cashews 56

Stuffed Jumbo Shells 56

Air Fried Crispy Chicken 57

Air Fried Chicken Bake 57

Air Fried Chicken And Sweet Potato 58

Air Fried Spinach Stuffed Chicken 58

Air Fried Chicken And Sweet Potatoes 59

Chapter 8: Beef Recipes 60

Air Fried Beef Rellenos 60

Air Fried Beef Meatloaf 60

Air fried Beef Meatballs 61

Air Fried Beef And Salad 61

Beef Fajitas 62

Beef With Herbs 62

Beef Teriyaki 63

Spicy Beef Steak 63

Beef Mignon With Herbs 63

Air Fried Beef Burgers 64

Air Fryer Greek Style Beef Chops 64

Air Fried Beef With Veggies 65

Air Fried Mongolian Beef 65

Air Fried Spare Ribs 66

Spicy Air Fried Steak With Mushrooms 66

Air Fried Beef Satay 66

Air Fried Steak With Pesto 67

Air Fried Beef Liver 67

Chapter 9: Lamb Recipes 68

Air Fryer Macadamia And Rosemary Crusted Lamb 68

Spicy Lamb 68

Lamb Burgers 69

Crusted Lamb With Orange 69

Stuffed Flat Bread With Lamb 70

Air Fried Lamb Ribs 70

Air Fried Lamb Koftas 71

Air Fried Lamb Chops With Herbs 71

Chapter 10: Pork Recipes 72

Air Fried Pork Sausage 72

Air Fried Pork With Cheese 72

Air Fried Stuffed Pork Chops With Cheese And Kale 72

Air Fried Pork Tenderloin With Paprika 73

Air Fried Teriyaki Pork Ribs 73

Air Fried Mustard Crusted Pork 74

Air Fried Pork With Vegetables 74

Air Fried Pork With Zucchini 75

Air Fried Italian Pork 75

Air Fried Pork 76

Air Fried Pork Chops With Sweet Potatoes 76

Air Fried Pork With Sake 77

Air Fried Pork Shoulder 77

Chapter 11: Fish And Seafood Recipes 78

Air Fried Halibut With Nuts 78

Air Fried Shrimp With Oregano 78

Air Fried Salmon With Soy Sauce 79

Air Fried Fish Nuggets 79

Air Fried Fish Fillets 79

Air Fried Tilapia 80

Air Fried Salmon With Panko Breadcrumbs. 80

Air Fried Coconut And Cheddar Cheese Shrimp 81

Air Fried Frozen Shrimp 81

Air Fried Fish And Chips 81

Air Fried Curried Prawns.................................82

Air Fried Scallops..82

Air Fried Fish Tacos 82

Air Fried Corn On The Cob With Lobsters.....83

Air Fried Squid Rings.......................................83

Chapter 12: Vegan Recipes.................84

Air Fried Tomato With Herbs........................84

Air Fried Cauliflower Bake 84

Air Fried Zucchini Patties With Cashew Cheese
....85

Air Fried Kale Nuggets....................................85

Air Fried Eggplant Fritters 86

Air Fried Veggies With Olive And Coriander .86

Chapter 13: Bread Recipes.................87

Whole Wheat Almond Bread 87

Walnut Bread 87

Crispy Vanilla Bread 87

Pumpkin And Cinnamon Swirl Bread 88

Air Fried Seed bread 88

Air Fried Rosemary Bread 89

Air Fried Brown Bread....................................89

Air Fried Garlic Bread......................................89

Air Fried Quick Bread 90

Air Fried Orange Almond Bread................... 90

Air Fried Butter Bread 91

Air Fried Foccacia Bread With Olives 91

Air Fried Garlic Bagels....................................92

Air Fried Sesame Buns...................................92

Air Fried Spicy Bagels.....................................93

Cheese Bread..93

Chapter 14: Dessert Recipes 94

Air Fried Flan...94

Air Fried Chocolate Bars.................................94

Air Fried Chocolate Muffins 95

Air Fried Vanilla Cake......................................95

Air Fried Raspberry Cobblers 95

Macadamia Biscuits 96

Cocoa And Vanilla Cupcakes 96

Air Fried Chocolate Ramekins........................97

Air Fried Orange Cake 97

Air Fried Glazed Donut...................................98

Air Fried Brownies 99

Air Fried Cocoa Cake 99

Air Fried Berry Brownies 100

Air Fried Chocolate Fudges 100

Air Fried Custard 100

Air Fried Blueberry Squares 101

Air Fried Cinnamon Cake 101

Air Fried Nut Clusters...................................102

Air Fried Honey Cookies...............................103

Air Fried Macaroons 103

Cooking Conversion Charts:............. 104

Alphabetical Index 106

INTRODUCTION

I'm Linda Roberts, a professional chef with an experience in air frying and baking. With more than ten years of experience in air frying, I am sharing with you the fruit of my experience. Indeed, my expertise lies in different aspects of food preparation, from chicken to burgers and sausages. Professionalism is my motto and you can be assured that your food will always be provided at the right temperature with my guidance. You won't regret so join me now on this read. Today, I want to thank you and congratulate you for downloading this book that I offer you. In this book, I will help you able to discover how simple it is to use a Classic Air Fryer to come up with a large myriad of delicious healthy recipes, and to cook at the same time your favourite dishes in a short time.

I guarantee that my cookbook will save you effort and time as well as ingredients. With the help of my cookbook, you will be able to reinvent recipes that you love very much and you will also rediscover the world of cooking with a revolutionary cooking appliance, Air Fryer. Using Air Fryer will change your cooking experience and your lifestyle for the better and for a healthier one. So what is so special about Air Fryer and why use it instead of any other cooking appliance?

Diversity and Versatility is the most important characteristics of using Air Fryers; and our recipes are not only diverse, but also healthy that displays a variety of dishes and different sumptuous and delicious techniques. The recipes you are going to discover will make a great choice for you during the weekend dishes, the holiday occasions and even in special occasions; everyone will find something they love in these recipes.

And whether you are a beginner to using air fryers or a professional cook; you will be able to use this book easily because of its easy – to – follow instructions and thanks to the simplicity of the ingredients this book uses. And if you are wondering why you should choose Air Frying instead of deep frying, the answer to that is easy, air frying is healthy and you can control the temperature of your air fryer with the automatic adjustment tool without burning it.

The functioning of an Air Fryer is not complicated at all, it all starts when your ingredients are in the cooking chamber; the hot air circulates around in the air fryer and allows cooking your meals in an easy way. And this is why air fryers have become the best choice for you to cook super delicious food recipes that will surprise you with its delicious taste. When you start using your own air fryer, you will be surprised with the delicious taste and healthiness of the recipe that you can get with the help of this innovative recipe cookbook that will make a great addition to your book shelf.

So, in short, Air fryers work more like an oven and it has many useful accessories like a basket and a double layer rack, and even if you are using an air fryer for the first time, you will easily learn how to use your air fryer with easy-to-follow instructions. Unlike deep frying, air frying food only needs one to two tablespoons of oil and this proves that air fried ingredients are healthy as well as tasty. My cookbook will offer you creative twists that will impress all of your family members and your friends; no one will notice the difference between deep fried and air fried food, because the taste will delicious, nutritious and crispy.

All of your favourite ingredients will be the heart our recipes. We are going to offer you some of the most delicious recipes you can imagine. And whether you prefer chicken crispy, fried potatoes, a quick crunchy breakfast recipe or some easy sides and snacks, you will find the recipes you are looking for and more. Thank you for choosing to purchase our book and thanks for reading it.

Chapter 1: Step-by-Step Air Frying

It is easy to operate, install and use a fryer. You only need to set two things for your Air Fryer, the temperature and the time. The rest is done for you by the Air fryer. However, many people still find it difficult to use their new air fryer for the first time. Which parameters and function buttons to use for which recipe? And that's understandable, because some air fryers are more complicated than they actually are. I'm going to give you some basic tips so you can start frying quickly and correctly.

Help, how do I install my Air fryer?

Air fryer works easily if you know the steps of using it and what you should and shouldn't do. Let's quickly run through the steps:

1. **Step 1: Un-boxing and checking**

You will find the air fryer in the box with lots of foam and plastic. Once you have removed all the packing material from the Air fryer, you can take a good look at the unit.

Carefully check the hot air fryer for any stickers. You must remove them from the Air fryer before using them. Do not use sticker remover or any other harsh solvents as they can permanently damage the exterior of the plastic. Also check the inside of the Air fryer. Open the drawer at the front and remove all packaging. It is also possible that the Air fryer basket still contains manual or other hidden documents.

2. **Step 2: Read the manual**

A manual is a bit boring to read, but I still recommend that you at least follow the manufacturer's advice for first use. Sometimes you won't find a complete manual. In this case, you should visit the official website of the manufacturer, as you can often download the manual there for free.

3. **Step 3: Cleaning the Air Fryer before using it:**

Remove the basket from the fryer. Clean the basket by hand in the sink with hot water and dish soap. Use a soft dish brush and especially no sharp objects. This could damage the Teflon non-stick coating.

4. **Step 4: The first test – Ready for take-off!**

Do not take your fries out of the freezer. We'll do a quick fryer test first. Plug it in and turn it on.

- *How to light a fryer?*

It depends on the brand and type. A digital fryer often needs to be turned on by pressing the on/off button. Then set the temperature to 180 degrees C/350°F and press start. It may be necessary to set a time, please consult your manual. A rotary knob fryer lights up when you set the timer. So if you turn the knob, which looks like a kind of timer, you will immediately notice that the Air fryer turns on.

- *Turn off the system after 30-60 seconds*

The test drive doesn't have to last long. This is just to test that your Air fryer is actually working.

- *Have you experienced any strange things?*

Has your Air fryer made a strange or rattling noise? Did your fryer turn off instantly? Or did something weird happen during the first use? Please contact the store or manufacturer directly.

5. **Step 5: A few other things to watch out for**

Let's say your new air fryer is in perfect working order. So, can you finally taste something from the deep fryer? Yes you can. So, take your chips or your favourite snack (or both) out of the freezer. I'm waiting for you.

Your First Air Fryer

Hope your frozen chips and snacks haven't thawed yet. Trying your fryer for the first time, the process is easy if you know the basic steps. Turn on your fryer and let it preheat, if necessary for your machine. I will briefly explain how to make good fries in the Air fryer through explaining how to use your Air Fryer for the first time:

1. Preheat the Air fryer to 180 degrees/355°F

2. Fill the Air fryer with frozen fries. It doesn't have to be special "air fries". I get good results with frozen fries.

3. Spread a layer of fries in the fryer basket. Don't completely fill your fries basket because you still need to be able to shake your fries. Either way, make sure your fries have room to move.

4.   Close the drawer and set your fryer for 15 minutes.

5.   After about 5 minutes you can check the status of the chips. Shake the fries by moving the fryer back and forth.

6.   Close the drawer to prevent the fryer from getting cold inside.

7.   After 5 minutes, check your fries again and give them a shake. Do they turn a little brown? If they are still shiny, you will have to be patient.

8.   Okay, now your fries have been in there for about 10 minutes at 180°C/355°F degrees. Depending on the thickness of your fries, they may be almost ready.

9.   Feel free to open your Air fryer drawer and check to see if the fries turn golden brown. When they're the right color you like, they're ready.

10.   Grab a bowl or your plate and shake the crispy fries out of the air fryer basket.

6.   Step 7: Clean your fryer in a blink of an eye:

Now that you have used your Air Fryer, there is another thing to pay attention to, and that is cleaning your Air fryer. What to do is very simple; all you need to do is to fill the pan with hot water. Then I add dish soap. You can soak this with the Air Fryer basket. Clean the pan and the basket in the sink. Just use a dish brush to remove crumbs and grease stains. Let the pan and basket dry on a draining rack. By cleaning your Air fryer and frying basket after each use, you can keep your Air fryer in top condition. Don't forget to check the inside of your deep fryer from time to time to see if there are food residues or splatters of grease. The interior can be cleaned carefully with a damp cloth.

AIR FRYER COOKING TIME:

Frozen Foods	Temperature °F	Time (minute)
Breaded Shrimp	395	9-10
Chicken Burger	355	11-12
Chicken Nuggets	365	11-13
Chicken Strips	375	14-16
Corn Dogs	395	8-10
Fish Filltes	385	12-14
Fish Sticks	395	11-13
French Fires	375	13-16

Chicken	Temperature °F	Time (minute)
Chickne Whole (3.5lbs)	355	40-55
Chicken Wings	375	25-28
Chicken Breast	385	11-14
Chicken Thighs	375	25-27

Beef	Temperature °F	Time (minute)
Rib Eye	400	11-13
Burgers	355	9-12
Filet Mignon	390	19-20
Meatballs	385	8-11

Pork	Temperature °F	Time (minute)
Bacon	345	12-14
Pork Chops	395	10-11
Sausages	385	8-12
Ribs	395	8-12

Fish & Seafood	Temperature °F	Time (minute)
Shrimp	365	6-8
Calamari	390	5-6
Scallops	395	6-7
Lobster Tails	375	4-6

Vegetables	Temperature °F	Time (minute)
Asparagus	395	6
Brussel Sprout	385	11-13
Green Beans	390	5-6
Corn	395	6

Chapter 2: Time Saving Hacks

Improvised cooking turns seemingly unrelated items from your refrigerator or closet into something appetizing. Improvised cooking consists of using convenient or ready-to-serve delicious dishes and adding fresh ingredients to personalize and complete the meal.

The great thing about improvised cooking is that some, or even most, of the work has already been done for you, so you spend minimal time in the kitchen. For recipe ideas, look for simplicity and speed. Pastas, sandwiches, stir-fries and soups can all be made in 10 minutes or less with ingredients you probably already have on hand.

For people who don't know what improvisational kitchen is, let me tell you that the improvised kitchen, or what is known as Speed Scratch, is becoming a widespread concept. At first, it was associated with the kitchen

of a caterer or a large restaurant, since the first stages of cooking were mainly prepared elsewhere, in a large kitchen, and the final dishes were completed on the premises of the event.

This cooking method is gaining so much popularity these days, and home cooks are embracing improvisational cooking and shaping it in their own way. The basic concept of improvised cooking is to use emergency or ready-made products and add fresh ingredients to personalize or complete the dish. Result: a homemade meal ready to eat in minutes, which is also good for your health.

When life has you on the run, the improvised kitchen can save you time while allowing you to feed your family well and do it with taste. Here are some tips to help you start cooking on the fly. And instead of coming home at the end of a long day, and the pantry is empty, and your first instinct will be to order. Instead, stock up on items like soups, pastas, beans, and canned vegetables. With one of these ingredients, or a combination of them, you can easily prepare a quick and healthy meal for you and your family.

Thinking fresh is the heart of improvisational kitchen; fresh herbs and veggies can transform any ready-made product into an amazing delicacy in no time. Thyme, oregano, and parsley are great starter herbs and can go with almost anything.

Chapter 3: A Week of Meal Prep

Planning your meals a week in advance can save you time, and you won't feel the stress of working and cooking at the same time and for that reason, here is a week of menus, planned for each day; of course you should adapt this menu according to your quota of points. Do not forget that you always have the possibility of consuming food to satiety and no more. But before starting our meal plan, here is the shopping list that you should use and have in your pantry before cooking.

SHOPPING LIST:

- Apples 5
- Bananas 8
- Grapefruits 2
- Oranges 5
- Broccoli 2 bunches
- Carrots 5 lbs
- Romaine lettuce 1
- Potatoes or
- Sweet potatoes 2 (or 1 large yam)
- Tomatoes 2
- Celery 1 branch
- White onion 5 lbs
- Green pepper 2
- Cabbage 2
- Green onion 1 bunch
- Mushrooms 4
- Garlic 1 head
- Canned
- Wax beans
- Fruit cocktail
- Sliced peaches
- Salsa* 1 small jar
- Tomatoes
- Tomato puree
- Tomato soup
- Frozen

CEREALS PRODUCTS:
- Whole wheat bread 1 loaf (for 2 weeks)
- Whole wheat bread rolls
- For 2 hamburgers (for 4 weeks)
- Whole Wheat Buns Pack of 6 (for 4 weeks)
- Whole wheat bagels Package of 6 (for 4 weeks)
- English muffins Pack of 6 (for 4 weeks)
- Whole Wheat Tortillas Package of 6 (for 4 weeks)
- Whole wheat pita bread Package of 6 (for 4 weeks)
- Whole wheat spaghetti
- Brown rice
- Whole wheat crackers* 1 box
- 1 pound of ground pork
- 2 pounds of ground beef
- ¼ pound of ground beef liver
- 2 Large cauliflower florets
- 1 Bunch of fresh basil
- 6 avocados
- An 10 oz packet of spinach leaves
- 3 cauliflowers
- 1 bunch of celery
- 2 packages of romaine lettuce hearts
- 1 red or yellow pepper
- 2 tomatoes
- 4 Granny smith apples
- Dairy products:
- 3 dozen eggs

- Thick cream
- ½ gallon of unsweetened milk
- 4 oz. grated parmesan cheese
- 8 oz packet pepper jack cheese slices
- 8 oz of sting cheese
- 8 oz of cream cheese
- Cheddar cheese
- 8 oz of sour cream   Spices
- 2 Heads of garlic
- Dried sage
- ginger

MILK AND ALTERNATIVES:
- Yogurt 1 pound (any flavor)
- Cheddar about 1 pound
- less (for the 4 weeks)
- Sour cream 250 ml (for 4 weeks),
- light
- Milk 4 l, skimmed, 1% or 2%
- MEAT AND ALTERNATIVES
- Pork ribs 2 (buy a pack of 6 and
- Freeze the rest for later)
- Chopped steak patties
- Frozen 2 (buy 1 box and you will have left over)
- Ground beef 2 pounds
- Eggs 2 dozen (for 4 weeks)
- Fish fillets, frozen,
- Salmon 1 pound
- Common beans, 1 pound
- Chickpeas 1 pound
- Nuts, unsalted 1 bag
- Peanut butter
- 8 cups Chicken stock

MEAL PLAN:

MONDAY:
Breakfast:
- Coffee with milk or an orange shake
- Liver and beef patties with eggs
- 1 portion of kiri
- 2 kiwis

Lunch:
- salad: 2 tomatoes + 1 small onion + parsley
- Pork chops with apple
- 1 pear

Dinner:
- 1 bowl of vegetable soup
- baked meat
- Salmon salad with red onion and granny smith apples

TUESDAY:
Breakfast
- tea or coffee
- 1 slice of wholemeal bread
- 1 boiled egg
- 2 kiwi

Lunch:
- Eggplant + onion + sliced green pepper in the oven + 1 teaspoon of olive oil
- Chicken cutlet with mushrooms + 2 tablespoons of 4% fresh cream.
- Cauliflower fried rice or stuffed vegan canelloni pasta
- 1/2 grapefruit

Dinner:
- Tomato salad + basil + hearts of palm + lettuce
- Quiche without dough with ham and cheese

WEDNESDAY:
Breakfast:
- coffee or tea
- 1 slice of wholemeal bread
- 2 teaspoons of fresh goat cheese
- 1 small bowl of cherries

Lunch:
- Chicken salad
- Plate of sausages with lentils

- 1 small slice of bread (if necessary)
- 1 yogurt

Dinner:
- Zucchini with cream
- 1 salmon steaks in the oven + lemon juice
- 2 to 3 spring rolls
- 1 fresh fruit salad without sugar

THURSDAY:
Breakfast:
- 1 cup of skimmed milk
- 1 slice of corn bread
- 2 teaspoons of light butter
- 1 banana + 1 kiwi
- 1 herbal tea of your choice 1 hour after the meal

Lunch:
- Green salad + cucumber + cherry tomato
- Spaghetti Bolognese
- 3 apples

Dinner:
- 1 bowl of coral lentil soup
- 1 pound of Air fried shrimp
  2 cups of sautéed rice with peas
  cheese + raspberry or strawberries

FRIDAY :
Breakfast:
- 1 tea or coffee without sugar
- 2 slices of sandwich bread
- 1 portion of cheese + 1 teaspoon of jam
- 1 fruit yoghurt 0%
- 2 clementines or 1 orange

Lunch:
- Asparagus with vinaigrette
- 2 slices of fresh baked tuna + pasta with broccoli and cream.
- 4 peaches

Dinner:
- Salad (carrot and shredded cabbage + vinaigrette)
- asparagus and mushroom omelet
- fresh pineapple + 1 sheep yoghurt

SATURDAY:
Breakfast:
- 3 cups of muesli
- 3 cups of skimmed milk
- 1 clementine
- 1 herbal tea without sugar 1 hour after the meal

Lunch:
- Tomato salad + mozzarella
- 1 plate of light salmon steak
- 100 g of cooked rice

Dinner:
- 1 bowl of vegetable soup
- 1 light tuna quiche
- 4 cups of grated cheese, feta
- 4 mangoes

SUNDAY:
Breakfast:
- coffee or tea with 2 pancakes + 2 sliced bananas and 1 tablespoon of maple syrup and % natural yoghurt

Lunch:
- Lentil or white bean salad
- 1 grilled chicken cutlet + celery puree
- 1 ½ cups of cottage cheese

Dinner:
- A fresh salad with cheese and fresh basil or parsley
- 2 pounds of lean veal
- 1 zucchini + 1 head of broccoli + 1 carrot sautéed with garlic and parsley.
- 1 yogurt 0%

Chapter 4: Breakfast Recipes

FLUFFY BREAKFAST DONUTS

Prep Time: 10 Minutes | Cooking Time: 12 Minutes | Servings: 3-4

INGREDIENTS

- 1 and ¾ cups of bread flour
- 1 and ¼ teaspoons of yeast
- 1 Tablespoon of sugar
- ½ Teaspoon of salt
- 6 Oz of hot water
- ¾ Tablespoon of raw agave nectar

DIRECTIONS

1. Start by adding all of your ingredients into a large and deep bowl; then you're your dry ingredients until it is very well blended
2. Gradually pour in the hot water while your blade is working and keep mixing
3. Form a ball from your dough and put it into an oiled bowl
4. Cover the bowl with a plastic wrap and set it aside for about 1 hour
5. Once your dough is ready, divide it into about 4 tiny balls
6. Flatten the balls and make a hole into the middle of each of it
7. Put a large pan filled to its half way with water over a medium high heat and when it starts boiling, add the agave and the bagels for about 30 seconds; flip the bagels and remove it from the boiling water
8. Dry your bagels with paper towels
9. Line the bagels over a greased baking tray that fits your air fryer basket; then close the lid
10. Set the timer to about 10 minutes and the temperature to 365° F
11. When the timer beeps; remove your bagels from the air fryer
12. Serve and enjoy your delicious breakfast donuts!

AIR FRIED GRIT PATTIES BREAKFAST

Prep Time: 12 Minutes | Cooking Time: 15 Minutes | Servings: 3

INGREDIENTS

- 1 Cup of minute grits
- 3 Cups of vegetable broth
- 2 Cubes of vegetable broth
- ½ Cup of frozen corn
- 1 Large minced jalapeno
- ¼ Cup of nutritional yeast

DIRECTIONS

1. In a deep and large pot, mix the water, the grits; the cubes of broth; the corn, and the jalapeno.
2. Let the ingredients boil over a medium-high heat; then make sure to constantly stir
3. Let simmer for around 4 minutes; then transfer your grits into a heat-proof bowl
4. Add the yeast and let the bowl cool for about 20 minutes; then put it in the refrigerator for about 10 minutes
5. Preheat your air fryer to about 350° F
6. Remove your mixture from the fridge and start scooping about ½ cup of the dollops of the grits and shape it into patties with your hand
7. Arrange your patties into a greased baking tray; then put it in the basket of your air fryer

8. Close the lid of the air fryer and set the timer to about 15 minutes and the temperature to about 365° F
9. When the timer beeps, remove the baking tray from the air fryer; and set the patties aside to cool for about 10 minutes; then remove it from the tray with a spatula
10. Serve and enjoy your grit patties!

BREAKFAST EGG MUFFINS

Prep Time: 10 Minutes | Cooking Time: 20 Minutes | Servings: 4

INGREDIENTS:

- 7 Oz of sliced leg ham
- 1 Pound of baby spinach
- 4 Large refrigerated eggs
- 4 Tablespoons of full cream milk
- 1 Tablespoon of olive oil
- 1 Tablespoon of unsalted butter
- 1 Pinch of salt
- 1 Pinch of ground black pepper

DIRECTIONS:

1. Preheat your air-fryer to a temperature of about 350°F.
2. Grease about 4 oven proof or steel ramekins with butter
3. Heat up a little bit of olive oil in a large pan and add to it the spinach and sauté for about 3 minutes
4. Drain off any excess of water
5. Divide the cooked spinach between your ramekins
6. Divide the sliced ham between your ramekins
7. In a separate bowl, crack in the eggs into each of the ramekins; then add 1 tablespoon of milk
8. Sprinkle 1 pinch of salt and 1 pinch of ground black pepper in the ramekins

9. Arrange the ramekins in the bottom of your air fryer and close the lid
10. Set the timer for about 15 to 20 minutes and the temperature to about 360°
11. When the time is up; turn off your air fryer
12. Serve and enjoy your egg muffins!

FRENCH TOAST WITH BLUEBERRIES

Prep Time: 10 Minutes | Cooking Time: 20 Minutes | Servings: 4

INGREDIENTS

- 3 and ½ tablespoons of unsalted butter
- 1 and ½ cups of whole milk
- 4 Large beaten eggs
- 1/3 Cup of granulated sugar
- 2 Teaspoons of vanilla pure extract
- ½ Teaspoon of kosher salt
- 12 Slices of white sandwich bread
- 1 Package of 6 Oz of small raspberries
- 1 Package of 6 Oz of blueberries

DIRECTIONS:

1. Preheat your air fryer for about 3 minutes
2. Grease 4 heat-proof ramekins on a temperature of about 300° F
3. In a large mixing bowl, mix the eggs with 1/3 cup of sugar; then add the vanilla, and the salt.
4. Now, time to remove the crusts from the slices of the bread
5. Brush the bread with the butter; then cut each of the pieces into triangles
6. Arrange slices of bread into the bottom of the ramekins; make sure to place the buttered side up
7. Top the ramekins with the berries
8. Repeat the same process more than once; then pour the mixture of the custard on top of the bread

9. Sprinkle a little bit of sugar over the bread and cover the ramekins with a foil
10. Place the ramekins in your air fryer and close the lid
11. Set the timer to about 20 minutes and the temperature to about 360°F
12. When the timer beeps, turn off your air fryer
13. Serve and enjoy your delicious French toast!

EGG ROLLS

Prep Time: 10 Minutes| Cooking Time: 15 Minutes | Servings: 4

INGREDIENTS

- ½ Tablespoon of Olive Oil
- 4 Large, peeled and cut Red Potatoes
- 1 Pinch of salt
- 1 Pinch of pepper
- 1 Cup of finely cut sausage
- 2 Large eggs
- 2 Cups of vegetable oil
- 8 to 9 Roll Wrappers
- 2 Tablespoons of water to seal the corners of the wrappers

DIRECTIONS:

1. Preheat your air fryer to about 350° F
2. Toss the diced potatoes in the basket of the air fryer and season it with salt and black pepper; then close the lid
3. Set the temperature to about 365° F and the timer to about 5 minutes
4. When the timer beeps, remove the potatoes from the air fryer
5. Whisk the eggs and the sausage; then season with a little bit of salt and toss it in a greased baking tray
6. Close the lid of the air fryer and set the timer to about 6 minutes and the temperature to about 5 minutes
7. When the timer beeps, remove the mixture from the air fryer and combine all the ingredients together
8. Assemble your egg rolls and start with the first wrapper
9. Spoon about 3 tablespoons of the filling into the wrapper, exactly into the middle of your wrapper; then fold a side of your wrapper over your filling
10. Press your wrapper as you roll it down; then repeat the same process with the remaining filling
11. Repeat the same process with the ingredients until you finish it all
12. Put the wrappers in the basket of the air fryer and close the lid
13. Set the timer to about 5 minutes and the temperature to about 365° F
14. When the timer beeps, remove the wrapper from the air fryer; then serve and enjoy it!

WHOLE MEAL CINNAMON TOAST

Prep Time: 10 Minutes| Cooking Time: 10 Minutes | Servings: 2-4

INGREDIENTS:

- 4 Slices of Whole meal Bread
- 2 Large and beaten eggs
- ¼ Cup of Whole Milk
- ¼ Cup of Brown Sugar
- 1 Tablespoon of honey
- 1 Teaspoon of Cinnamon
- 1 Pinch Nutmeg
- 1 Pinch Icing Sugar

DIDIRECTIONS:

1. Chop up the bread slices into about three sticks
2. Put the remaining ingredients in a large mixing bowl and combine very well.

3. Dip each of your bread sticks into your mixture and put it in your air fryer
4. When you finish with the 16 sticks, arrange the sticks in the air fryer and bake it at a temperature of about 325° F and set the timer for around 10 minutes
5. Flip the bread sticks once through the cooking process
6. Once the timer beeps, serve and enjoy your delicious French stick toasts.
7. Serve your sticks with icing sugar and with berries!

GRANOLA BREAKFAST

Prep Time: 10 Minutes | Cooking Time: 10 Minutes | Servings: 3

INGREDIENTS:

- 1 and ½ cups of mixed nuts
- ¼ Cup of sesame seeds
- ¼ Cup of pumpkin seeds
- 1/3 Cup of sunflower seeds
- ½ Cup of coconut flakes
- 2 Tablespoons of vegetable oil
- 1 Teaspoon of ground cinnamon
- 1 Teaspoon of ground ginger
- 2 Mashed bananas; better to use mashed bananas

DIRECTIONS:

1. Pour the vegetable oil in a large – sized baking tray that fits your air fryer
2. Preheat your air fryer to 325 degree Fahrenheit and put the baking tray in the basket steamer to heat up
3. Combine the seeds, the nuts and the coconut flakes
4. Remove your tray from the air fryer and put the nuts, the seeds and the coconut flakes in the heated tray
5. Put the tray in the air fryer and close the lid
6. Set the time to about 5 minutes and the heat to 325° F; meanwhile, peel your banana and chop it
7. Mash the banana with a fork
8. When the time beeps, remove the mixture of nuts from the air fryer and add the mashed banana to it
9. Bake the granola for 5 more minutes
10. Once the timer beeps, remove from the air fryer; add the ginger and the ground cinnamon
11. Serve and enjoy your granola breakfast!

AIR FRIED MUSHROOM FRITTATA

Prep Time: 5 Minutes | Cooking Time: 6 Minutes | Servings: 2-4

INGREDIENTS:

- 1 Cup of egg whites
- 2 Tablespoon of skim milk
- ¼ Cup of sliced tomato
- ¼ Cup of sliced mushrooms
- 2 Tablespoons of chopped fresh chives
- 1 Pinch of black pepper

DIRECTIONS:

1. Preheat your Air Fryer at a temperature of about 320° F.
2. Combine all your ingredients in a large bowl
3. Pour your batter in the pan provided with your air fryer
4. Bake the Frittata in your air fryer for about 15 minutes
5. When the time is up; turn off your air fryer
6. Slice the Frittata
7. Serve and enjoy your delicious Frittata!

AIR FRIED PECAN OAT BREAKFAST

Prep Time: 7 Minutes| Cooking Time: 20 Minutes | Servings:: 2-3

INGREDIENTS

- 2 Cups of quick-cook oats
- 1 Teaspoon of baking powder
- 1 Teaspoon of cinnamon
- ¼ Teaspoon of salt
- ⅓ Cup of packed brown sugar
- To make the wet mixture:
- 2 Cups of non-fat milk
- 2 Large eggs
- ½ Tablespoon of vanilla extract
- 3 Tablespoons of honey
- 1 and ½ tablespoons of melted butter
- 2 Cups of frozen mixed berries
- ¼ Cup of separated pecans

DIRECTIONS:

1. Preheat your air fryer to a temperature of about 375° F for about 3 minutes
2. In a large bowl, mix the oats with the baking powder, the cinnamon, the brown sugar and the salt; then set it aside
3. In a large bowl, mix the milk, the eggs, the vanilla, the honey and the butter
4. Layer about half of the berries in the air fryer baking dish and top it with the mixture of the dry oats
5. Place the baking dish in your air fryer and bake for about 15 to 20 minutes
6. When the time is up, slice the baked oatmeal
7. Serve and enjoy your baked oatmeal

BREAKFAST HASH BROWNS

Prep Time: 10 Minutes| Cooking Time: 20 Minutes | Servings: 3

INGREDIENTS

To make the filling
- 1 and ½ tablespoons of olive Oil
- 1 Small diced Onion
- 4 to 5 finely chopped Garlic cloves
- 4 Sliced pork sausages
- 2 Large grated potatoes with the skin removed
- 1 Cup of roughly chopped Spinach
- ½ Teaspoon of Chilli Flakes
- 1 Teaspoon of Dried Sage
- 1 Teaspoon of Dried Thyme

To make the custard
- 1/3 Cup of whole Milk
- 1 Large egg
- ½ Cup of finely grated smoked cheddar cheese

DIRECTIONS:

1. Preheat your air fryer to about 360° F
2. Grease the baking dish of your air fryer with a little bit of butter
3. Now, prepare the filling by heating the oil in a large frying pan
4. Add the garlic and the onion; then sauté for about 2 minutes
5. Add the sliced sausages and cook for 1 additional minute
6. Add in the grated potatoes and the spinach; then sauté for about 2 other minutes
7. Add the herbs and the seasoning
8. In a separate bowl, crack in the eggs and whisk very well
9. Gradually add the milk and mix very well

10. Add the seasoning and mix the cheese; then stir
11. Place the filling of the potato in your baking tray
12. Pour the custard over the potatoes
13. Sprinkle a little bit of cheese on top
14. Place the baking dish in the air fryer and close the lid
15. Bake your dish for about 20 minutes at a temperature of about 375° F
16. When the time is up, serve and enjoy your delicious breakfast!

SAUSAGE BREAKFAST

Prep Time: 10 Minutes| Cooking Time: 15 Minutes | Servings: 3

INGREDIENTS:

- 1 Pound of lean ground chicken
- ½ Teaspoon of garlic powder
- ½ dash of ground black pepper
- 1 Teaspoon of dried sage
- 1 Teaspoon of crushed red pepper flakes
- 1 Teaspoon of dried oregano
- 1 dash of Kosher salt

DIRECTIONS:

1. Preheat your air fryer to about 350° F
2. Combine your ingredients altogether into a large bowl and make your sausage patties to your desired thickness and size.
3. Arrange your patties in the basket of the air fryer and close the lid
4. Set the timer to about 10 to 15 minutes
5. Once the timer beeps, remove the patties from the air fryer; then serve and enjoy your breakfast!

FLAT BREAKFAST BREAD

Prep Time: 10 Minutes| Cooking Time: 10 Minutes | Servings: 5

INGREDIENTS

- 1 and ½ teaspoons of active dry yeast
- 1 and ½ teaspoons of unrefined cane sugar
- ½ Teaspoon of kosher salt
- 1 and ½ cups of all-purpose flour
- 1 and ½ cups of whole spelt flour
- 1 Tablespoon of finely cut fresh rosemary leaves
- 2 Tablespoons of extra-virgin olive oil
- 2 Tablespoons of thyme
- ½ Cup of pitted and cut olive

DIRECTIONS:

1. In a deep mixing bowl, mix a little bit of olive oil with a little bit of yeast, salt, sugar and pour in about 1 cup of water (Make sure the water is warm)
2. Set the mixture aside to rest for about 11 minutes
3. Add in the flours and the chopped rosemary; then blend the ingredients together on a very low speed
4. Use the dough hook in order to knead your dough; and once you obtain a smooth one; divide it into about 2 balls
5. Put the dough balls over a floured baking paper and let rest for about 3 hours
6. Put the pizza over a greased baking tray and use your hands and fingers to spread it to a circle
7. Cover your bread with a kitchen towel and set it aside to rest for about 12 minutes
8. Brush the bread with olive oil and put it in the basket of the air fryer; then close the lid and set the timer to about 10 minutes and the temperature to about 365° F

9. When the timer beeps, remove the bread from the air fryer and sprinkle a little bit of pepper, olive oil and salt
10. Serve and enjoy!

EGGS IN AVOCADO

Prep Time:: 10 minutes, cook time: 18 minutes; Serves 2

INGREDIENTS:

- 1 Teaspoon of vegetable oil
- 1 Ripe avocado
- 2 Large organic eggs
- 1 Pinch of salt
- 1 Pinch of pepper
- Chopped walnuts
- Use fresh thyme

DIRECTIONS:

1. Preheat your air fryer to about 385°F and grease a baking tray that fits your air fryer basket with cooking spray
2. Cut your avocado into halves and remove its pit; then scoop out the flesh of the avocado
3. Remove a tiny part of the avocado skin and set it aside
4. In medium bowl; crack your eggs and split it into about 3 small bowls or container
5. Put the egg yolks into glass tea cups and the white yolk into another bowl
6. Add the salt and the pepper
7. Grease a baking tray that fits your air fryer with cooking spray
8. In a shallow, large skillet; sear the avocado halves for about 30 seconds
9. Line the avocados in the baking tray; and fill its cavities with a little bit of egg whites; then evenly divide the egg yolks between the avocado halves and season it with salt and pepper
10. Put the lid of avocados on and put the baking tray in the air fryer; then close the lid
11. Set the temperature to about 350° F and the timer to about 18 minutes
12. When the timer beeps, remove the lid of the air fryer and serve your avocado boats with thyme, and walnuts

WHOLE WHEAT BANANA TOAST

Prep Time: 10 Minutes| Cooking Time: 13 Minutes | Servings: 3

INGREDIENTS

- 1 Loaf of sliced whole wheat bread
- 2 Ripe bananas
- 1 Can of milk
- 2 Teaspoons of vanilla
- 1 Teaspoon of cinnamon
- ¼ Teaspoon of salt
- ½ Cup of dry roasted pecans
- Cooking spray

DIRECTIONS

1. Start by cutting the whole-wheat bread into equal-sized slices
2. In a blender; mix the milk, the pecan, the vanilla, the cinnamon and the salt Pour your obtained mixture into a deep bowl; then add the bread and let soak for about 2 minutes
3. Grease a baking tray and preheat your air fryer to about 350° F
4. Lay the soaked bread into the greased tray and put it in the basket of the air fryer
5. Close the lid and set the timer to about 8 minutes and the temperature to 360°F
6. When the timer beeps, remove the bread toasts from the air fryer; then set it aside to cool for about 5 minutes

7. Serve and enjoy with maple syrup!

AIR FRIED PANCAKES

Prep Time: 10 Minutes | Cooking Time: 5 Minutes | Servings: 2-4

INGREDIENTS:

- ½ Tablespoon of butter
- 2 Large eggs
- 2.5 Oz of cream cheese
- 1 ½ cups of all purpose flour

DIRECTIONS:

1. In a medium bowl, mix the cream cheese with the eggs and the flour; then keep whisking until it becomes fluffy and creamy
2. Let the batter aside for about 4 minutes
3. Grease the air fryer baking tray with cooking spray and pour in 1 tea cup of the pancake batter
4. Put the baking tray in the basket of your air fryer; then close the lid
5. Set the temperature to about 365° F and the timer to about 5 minutes
6. When the timer beeps, remove the pancake from the air fryer
7. Repeat the same process to make the number of pancake until your run out of butter
8. Serve and enjoy your pancakes!

CLOUD PANCAKES

Prep Time: 10 Minutes | Cooking Time: 24 Minutes | Servings: 4

INGREDIENTS:

- 3 Separated Large eggs
- 3 Tablespoons of cream cheese
- 3 Tablespoons of chopped scallions; green onions or you can use chives
- ½ Teaspoon of white or black pepper
- 1 Pinch of sea salt
- 1 Teaspoon of white vinegar
- 2 Tablespoons of vegetable oil

DIRECTIONS:

1. Preheat your air fryer to about 300° F
2. Grease a baking paper with 1 tablespoon of oil and set it aside
3. Separate the eggs and make sure that you don't see yolks in the egg whites
4. Add the whites of eggs to a bowl and put the egg yolks into another bowl
5. Add the scallion, the cream cheese, the pepper and the salt to the egg yolks and set it aside.
6. Add about 1 teaspoon of the white vinegar to the whites of eggs whites and add 1 pinch of salt if needed
7. Whisk the egg whites on a high speed and set it aside
8. Combine the mixture of yolks
9. Pour the mixture of yolks into the whites; but be careful not to over mix.
10. With a wooden spoon, scoop about ¼ cup of mixture and make the shape of rounds on the baking paper (Make the rounds about the size of a cookie or a little bit larger)
11. Using a large spoon or a quarter cup, scoop the mixture into even rounds on the sheet; make sure to leave a small room between the rounds and put the baking sheet in a baking tray
12. Put the baking tray in the air fryer basket and close the lid
13. Set the temperature to about 320° F and the timer to 24 minutes
14. When the timer beeps, remove the baking tray from the air fryer; then serve and enjoy your breakfast!

Chapter 5: Snack and Appetizers Recipes

AIR FRIED BRUSSELS SPROUTS

Prep Time: 8 Minutes| Cooking Time: 20Minutes | Servings: 4

INGREDIENTS:

- 2 Pounds of halved and trimmed Brussels sprouts; remove the outer leaves
- 2 Tablespoons of melted vegetable oil
- 1 Teaspoon of dry ketchup spice
- ¾ Teaspoon of fine sea salt
- 1 Pinch of freshly ground black pepper

DIRECTIONS:

1. Preheat your air fryer to about 390° F; then line a baking sheet with aluminium foil tin or with parchment paper
2. Trim then ends of the sprouts; then slice it into a lengthwise way
3. Put the sprouts in a large and deep bowl; then drizzle with oil and toss it very well with your hands
4. Add a little bit of salt with Ketchup spice
5. Put the Brussels sprouts above your baking sheet and sprinkle with black pepper
6. Put the baking sheet in the basket of the air fryer and close the lid
7. Set the timer to about 20 minutes and the temperature to 365° F
8. When the timer beeps, remove the Brussels sprouts from the air fryer; then serve and enjoy its crispy taste with salad or rice!

AIR FRIED EGGPLANTS WITH ZAATAR

Prep Time: 10 Minutes| Cooking Time: 7 Minutes | Servings: 6

INGREDIENTS:

- 1 Pound of eggplants
- 1 Tablespoon of vegetable oil
- 1 Tablespoon of Maggi seasoning sauce.
- 1 teaspoon of onion powder
- 1 Teaspoon of garlic powder
- 1 teaspoon of Sumac
- 3 Tablespoons of Za'atar
- 2 Bay leaves
- ½ piece of Lemon
- 1 Tablespoon of Olive oil

DIRECTIONS:

1. Take the eggplants first and wash it thoroughly. Separate the stem and cut the eggplants into small cubes of 2 cm in size.
2. Heat olive oil using a microwave and pour it into a large mixing bowl along with sumac, Maggi, za'atar, garlic powder, onion powder and stir to mix properly with each other. Add the eggplant cubes into the bowl and toss well. If you want to add more olive oil or 1 tsp of oil you can add it.
3. Take the cooking basket from the air fryer and place the mixture into it. Set the temperature of the air fryer to 3200F and cook for 15 minutes. After that raise the temperature to 3500F and roast the items for last 5 to 6 minutes or more as you want the texture.

AIR FRIED POTATO SKINS

Prep Time: 10 Minutes| Cooking Time: 30 Minutes | Servings: 4

INGREDIENTS:

- 6 large Yukon Gold potatoes
- 7 cooked and crumbled bacon pieces, fat reserved
- 2 1/2 cups shredded sharp cheddar cheese
- 1/2 cup thinly sliced scallions
- ¼ cup of sour cream
- 1 pinch of salt to taste

DIRECTIONS:

1. Wash and pierce the potatoes with a paring knife. Place the potatoes on a large, microwave-safe platter in a single layer.
2. Wrap the potatoes with a damp paper towel, and microwave for 5 minutes on high heat
3. Turn the potatoes over. Microwave the potatoes for another 5 to 7 minutes, or until soft.
4. Refrigerate the potatoes for about 20 minutes to allow them to cool.
5. Cut the potatoes in half lengthwise. Scoop out the insides, saving the cooked potato for subsequent use in mashed potatoes.
6. Inside the potato, leave about a 1/4-inch from the skins; then brush the saved bacon grease inside the potato skins.
7. Place six of the skins, skin side down, in the air fryer basket.
8. Cook for about 10 minutes at 400°F. Open the basket and stuff the skins with the shredded cheddar cheese. Return to the oven for 3 - 4 minutes, or until the cheese is melted and bubbling. Repeat with the rest of the potato skins.
9. To serve, top the cooked potato skins with the cooked bacon, scallions, and sour cream. If necessary, season with salt.
10. Enjoy your potato skins!

CRISPY FETA CHEESE FRIES

Prep Time: 5 Minutes| Cooking Time: 6 Minutes | Servings: 4

INGREDIENTS:

- 2 Egg yolks
- 8 Oz of Feta cheese
- 2 Tablespoons of thinly chopped parsley
- 2 tbsp of thinly chopped
- 1 finely chopped scallion
- 2 sheets, frozen and defrosted filo pastry
- 2 tbsp of olive oil
- 1 pinch of ground black pepper

DIRECTIONS:

1. Take the egg yolk in a mixing bowl and beat it well. Add the feta cheese, scallion and parsley and mix all together. Add a pinch of pepper to taste. Now, take the filo onto the cutting board and cut each sheet of filo into three strips. Place a teaspoon of feta cheese mixture on a side of pastry and fold the tip to make the triangle. Make the triangle in such a way that the filling is wrapped totally and securely by the pastry. Do it for all the filling remains.
2. Just set the temperature of the air fryer to 390°F and prepare it for cooking. Take the triangles and brush oil lightly on the both surface of each triangle and arrange them into the cooking basket of the air fryer. Cook up to 6 triangles at a time. Cook for 3 minutes at 390°F and then lower the temperature to 360°F and cook for another 3 minutes.
3. You are done, serve hot and enjoy your appetizer!

BROCCOLI FRITTERS

Prep Time: 10 Minutes| Cooking Time: 12 Minutes | Servings: 6

INGREDIENTS:

- 2 and ½ cups of broccoli
- ¼ Cup of chopped onion
- ¼ Cup of packed cilantro
- ⅓ Teaspoon of salt
- ½ Teaspoon of garlic powder
- ½ Teaspoon of paprika
- 1 Teaspoon of pepper powder
- 1 Teaspoon of olive oil
- 1 Tablespoon of barbecue sauce
- ¾ Cup of all purpose flour

DIRECTIONS:

1. Start by pulsing the broccoli florets, the onion and the cilantro into a food processor.
2. Transfer the pulsed ingredients into a large bowl; then add the rest of your ingredients and mix very well
3. Set your mixture aside for about 2 minutes and you can add a little bit more of flour if you notice it is too runny
4. Shape your batter when into about 6 patties
5. Grease a baking tray with cooking spray; then line the patties in it
6. Put the tray in the basket of the air fryer; and close the lid
7. Set the temperature to about 375° F and the timer to about 12 minutes
8. When the timer beeps; remove your fritters from the air fryer
9. Serve the fritters!

AIR FRIED MUSHROOMS

Prep Time: 8 Minutes| Cooking Time: 25 Minutes | Servings: 4-6

INGREDIENTS:

- 1 ½ Pounds of Mushrooms
- 1 Tablespoon of Olive oil or olive oil
- ½ Teaspoon of Garlic powder
- 2 Tablespoons of white vermouth

DIRECTIONS:

1. Take the mushrooms first and wash it thoroughly in flowing water. Put them into a salad spinner when they are dried and spin. Pour the spun mushrooms onto a plate and divide it into quarter. Set aside.
2. In a paddle types air fryer, put the garlic powder, the olive oil in the pan. Heat the ingredients for 2 minutes. While heating, stir the ingredients by using a wooden spoon from preventing clumped.
3. Now add the mushrooms and heat it for 25 to 30 minutes. After that add the white vermouth with the mushrooms and cook a little of approximately 5 minutes.
4. You can serve this item with garlic meat items like beef steak or lamb etc.

AIR FRIED POTATOES

Prep Time: 10 Minutes| Cooking Time: 15 Minutes | Servings: 4

INGREDIENTS:

- 2 Large peeled and sweet potatoes; cut into sticks of 4 inch each
- 3 Tablespoons of Olive Oil
- ½ Teaspoon of black Pepper
- ¼ Teaspoon of Cayenne Pepper
- ¼ Teaspoon of Paprika
- ¼ Teaspoon of Cumin

- ¼ Teaspoon of Garlic Powder

DIRECTIONS:

1. Preheat your air fryer to about 390° F
2. Put the sweet potatoes in a large and deep bowl; then drizzle with oil
3. Add your spices and stir very well until your ingredients are very well- mixed.
4. Put the pieces of the sweet potatoes in the basket of the air fryer and close the lid
5. Set the timer to about 15 minutes and the temperature to about 390° F
6. When the timer beeps, remove the potatoes from the air fryer
7. Serve and enjoy your delicious air fried potatoes!

AIR FRIED BROCCOLI FLORETS WITH SESAME SEEDS

Prep Time: 10 Minutes| Cooking Time: 20 Minutes | Servings: 6

INGREDIENTS:

- 1 Large head of broccoli
- 1 Tablespoon of olive oil
- Half a lemon
- 1 Teaspoon of Garlic powder
- 1 Teaspoon of sesame seeds

DIRECTIONS:

1. At first wash the broccoli with water. Cut it into bite size or the size you like. Dry it up and set aside.
2. Heat olive oil using a microwave for 2 minutes.
3. Now, take a large mixing bowl and add the olive oil along with the broccoli and lemon juice. Mix all together properly.
4. Set the temperature of the air fryer to 3200F to preheat it. Place the broccoli mixture with vegetable oil into the cooking basket of the air fryer and cook for 15 to 20 minutes. Remove the basket from the air fryer and sprinkle the sesame seeds over the broccoli and cook for the last 5 minutes to allow toasting the seeds.
5. Serve when it is hot, and enjoy your appetizer!

AIR FRIED AVOCADO

Prep Time: 8 Minutes| Cooking Time: 13 Minutes | Servings: 5

INGREDIENTS

- 4 Small peeled avocados
- ¼ Teaspoon of garlic powder
- ¼ Teaspoon of salt
- ¼ Cup of garbanzo flour
- ½ Cup of milk
- 1 Cup of breadcrumbs

DIRECTIONS:

1. Preheat your air fryer to about 390° F
2. Grease a baking pan that fits your air fryer basket, with cooking spray
3. Start by cutting the avocados into slices
4. Mix the salt, the garlic and the flour in a large bowl; then pour the milk in another dish
5. Coat each of the avocados into the flour
6. Dip each slice of avocado into the milk
7. Sprinkle the breadcrumbs over the slices and press it down
8. Line the slices of avocado into the already greased and prepared baking pan; then put it in the basket of the air fryer and close the lid
9. Set the timer to about 13 minutes and the temperature to about 375° F
10. When the timer beeps, remove the tray from the air fryer, then set it aside for about 5 minutes

POTATO CHIPS

Prep Time: 5 Minutes| Cooking Time: 30 Minutes | Servings: 4-6

INGREDIENTS:

- 2 Pounds of Potatoes
- 1 tbsp of olive oil or any vegetable oil of your choice
- 1 Pinch of sea salt

DIRECTIONS:

1. Take the potatoes first. Wash with clean water and peel it. Place onto a cutting board and cut into thin slices. You can use blade type knife or your mandolin to do that.
2. After slicing the potatoes take those to a large bowl with full of cold water. Wet the slices for a couple minutes. The water in which the slices immerging will help to prevent discoloration of the chips due to air contact.
3. Take the potato slices into the basket of the air fryer and set the temperature to 350°F. Preheat the air fryer first. Spread one tablespoon of vegetable oil over the chips into the cooking basket and shake very well.
4. Cook for 30-45 minutes but not at a time. Continuously check the chips at an interval of 10 minutes. When the potato chips are brown in color, remove the basket from the air fryer and pour the chips in a serving bowl.
5. Serve and enjoy your potato chips!

STUFFED AVOCADO

Prep Time: 10 Minutes| Cooking Time: 15 Minutes | Servings: 4

INGREDIENTS:

- 6 Medium avocados
- 1 ½ Cups of uncooked lentils
- 1 Cup of bread crumbs
- Leaves of parsley
- 1 Pinch of salt

DIRECTIONS:

1. Start by cooking the lentils in 1 cup of boiling water over a high heat
2. Pulse your lentils in a food processor
3. Mix the breadcrumbs with the mixture of the lentils
4. Add 1 teaspoon of sauce of mustard; then season the ingredients with the salt and the pepper and set the mixture aside for about 10 minutes; meanwhile; prepare your avocados
5. Cut the avocado into halves in a lengthwise way; then gently remove the skin and the stone from its inside.
6. Cover the halves of the avocados with the mixture of the lentils; then put the halves on top of each other in order to make the form of a bowl in each half
7. Combine the parsley with the breadcrumbs and mix very well; then roll your Scotch eggs into the mixture of the breadcrumbs and the parsley
8. Line the avocados on a baking sheet lined with the parchment paper; then put it in the air fryer basket and close the lid
9. Set the timer to about 16 minutes and the temperature to around 345° F
10. When the timer beeps, remove your stuffed avocado from the air fryer; then set it aside for about 10 minutes to cool
11. Serve and enjoy!

STUFFED MUSHROOMS

Prep Time: 10 Minutes| Cooking Time: 15 Minutes | Servings: 4-5

INGREDIENTS:

- 4 to 5 large Portobello mushroom caps
- 1 Tbsp of olive oil
- 7 Ounces of sausage patties

- 4 Large beaten eggs
- ¼ Cup of diced basil
- 2 Tablespoons of diced chives
- 1 Pinch of Kosher salt
- 1 Pinch of pepper
- ½ Cup of shredded sharp cheddar cheese

DIRECTIONS:

1. Preheat your air fryer to a temperature of about 200°C/400° F
2. Spray your air fryer pan with cooking spray
3. Remove the stem and the gills from the mushrooms and make sure to fill the mushrooms with the eggs
4. Rub the inside of the mushrooms with a little bit of olive oil
5. Brown the sausage and break up the patties in a large fryer
6. Add the eggs, the basil and the chives; then mix very well
7. Fill each half of the mushrooms with 1 tablespoon of the mixture
8. Arrange the mushrooms in your air fryer pan; then sprinkle with cheese
9. Place the baking pan in your air fryer and lock the lid
10. Set the timer to about 15 minutes and the temperature to about 350° F
11. When the timer beeps; turn off your Air Fryer; then remove the pan from your air fryer
12. Serve and enjoy your delicious appetizer!

AIR FRIED ONION

Prep Time: 5 Minutes| Cooking Time: 5 Minutes | Servings: 4

INGREDIENTS:

- 5 Tablespoons of dry breadcrumbs
- 1 Teaspoon of seasoning salt
- 1/8 Teaspoon of pepper
- 2 Tablespoons of grated Parmesan cheese
- ½ sliced sweet onion
- 1 Slightly beaten egg white
- 2 tbsp of cooking spray

DIRECTIONS:

1. Combine the crumbs, the salt, the pepper and the Parmesan cheese in a small bowl.
2. Dip the onion rings into the egg white and then into the breadcrumbs.
3. Place the onion rings in your air fryer basket.
4. Spray the onions with your cooking spray on both sides
5. Close the lid of the air fryer and seal it tightly; then set the timer to 5 minutes and the temperature to 380° F
6. When the timer beeps, unplug the air fryer; then serve and enjoy your crispy onion rings!

AIR FRIED CHEESE STICKS

Prep Time: 7 Minutes| Cooking Time: 10 Minutes | Servings: 4

INGREDIENTS

- 10 Strings of diced cheeses
- 2 Beaten eggs
- 1 Cup of Parmesan cheese
- 1 tbsp of Italian seasoning
- 1 Minced garlic clove

DIRECTIONS:

1. Combine the Parmesan cheese with the Italian seasoning and the minced garlic in a bowl.
2. Dip each of the cheese strings in the mixture of the egg and mix very well
3. Roll the strings in the cheese crumbs again.
4. Gently press the cheese crumbs with your fingers

5. Put the coated cheese in the refrigerator for about 1 hour
6. Preheat your Air Fryer to a temperature of about 375° F
7. Spray your air fryer pan with cooking spray
8. Arrange the cheese strings in your Air Fryer pan
9. Place the baking pan in your Air Fryer and lock the lid
10. Set the timer for about 8 to 9 minutes and set the temperature to about 365° F
11. When the timer beeps; turn off your Air Fryer; then remove the baking pan and let the cheese sticks cool for about 5 minutes
12. Serve and enjoy your cheese sticks!

AIR FRIED ASPARAGUS

Prep Time: 7 Minutes| Cooking Time: 10 Minutes | Servings: 6

INGREDIENTS:

- 1 Cup of Panko bread
- ½ Cup of shredded cheese of your choice
- 1 Pinch of salt
- 1 Pinch of ground, black pepper
- 1 Pound of trimmed asparagus
- ¼ Cup of all-purpose flour
- 3 Tablespoons of peanut butter

DIRECTIONS:

1. Preheat your air fryer to 390° F
2. Grease a baking tray with a little bit of cooking spray
3. In a large and deep bowl, mix altogether the Panko and the cheese of your choice; then season it with a little bit of salt and 1 pinch of black pepper
4. Dredge the asparagus into the flour, then in the peanut butter and then in the mixture of the Panko
5. Line the asparagus in the greased baking tray; then put it in the air fryer basket and close the lid
6. Set the timer to 11 minutes and the temperature to about 375° F
7. When the timer beeps, remove the asparagus from the air fryer
8. Serve and enjoy your air fried asparagus!

AIR FRIED RADISH

Prep Time: 8 Minutes| Cooking Time: 12 Minutes | Servings: 4

INGREDIENTS

- 1 pound of fresh radishes
- 2 tbsp of vegetable oil
- ½ tsp of sea salt
- ½ tsp of pepper

DIRECTIONS:

1. Preheat your Air Fryer to a temperature of about 400 degrees F.
2. Slice the radishes into thin slices
3. Place the radish slices in a bowl and toss it with oil
4. Lay the radishes in the Air Fryer basket
5. Whisk the pepper and the salt together; then sprinkle it over the radishes
6. Lock the lid of your Air Fryer and set the timer for about 12 minutes
7. Set the temperature to about 200° C/400° F
8. When the timer beeps; turn off your Air Fryer
9. Remove the pan from the air fryer
10. Serve and enjoy your air fried radishes!

AIR FRIED GREEN BEANS

Prep Time: 5 Minutes| Cooking Time: 12 Minutes | Servings: 4

INGREDIENTS

- 1 pound of fresh green beans
- 1 Large egg
- 2 tbsp of olive oil
- ¼ Cup of flour
- ¼ Cup of Parmesan cheese
- 1 tsp of sea salt
- 1 tsp of garlic powder
- ½ tsp of paprika
- 1 Dash of pepper

DIRECTIONS:

1. Preheat your Air Fryer to a temperature of about 200°C/400° F
2. Line the Air Fryer baking pan with aluminium and drizzle it with a little bit of olive oil.
3. Wash the beans and trim it and set it aside
4. Beat the olive oil with the egg
5. Coat the green beans with the egg mixture
6. Mix the rest of the ingredients in a separate bowl; then toss the beans into it
7. Place the green beans in the air fryer basket
8. Lock the lid of your Air Fryer and set the timer to about 12 minutes
9. When the timer beeps; turn off your Air Fryer; then serve and enjoy your Air fried green beans!

AIR FRIED APPLE CHIPS

Prep Time: 5 Minutes| Cooking Time: 10 Minutes | Servings: 2-4

INGREDIENTS:

- 6 apples
- 1 teaspoon cinnamon

DIRECTIONS:

1. To begin, wash and dry the apples. After they have dried, cut them into thin slices, approximately 18 inch thick, with a mandolin or a sharp knife.
2. Sprinkle a teaspoon of cinnamon on the apple slices and arrange them in a single layer in the air fryer basket.
3. Set the temperature to 380 degrees F and cook time to 8-10 minutes after they're in the basket.
4. After 5 minutes, flip the slices. Allow the slices to crisp for at least 5 minutes. Rest periods of 15-30 minutes are ideal.
1. Serve and enjoy your apple chips!

WRAPPED HALLOUMI CHEESE WITH BACON

Prep Time: 5 Minutes| Cooking Time: 12 Minutes | Servings: 4

INGREDIENTS:

- 8 Oz of Halloumi cheese
- 5 Oz of sliced bacon

DIRECTIONS:

2. Preheat your Air Fryer to a temperature of about 200° C/400° F
3. Cut the cheese into about 8 to 10 pieces.
4. Wrap each pieces of cheese with a bacon piece
5. Line your Air Fryer pan with a baking sheet
6. Arrange the bacon cheese wraps in the pan
7. Place the pan in your Air Fryer and lock the lid
8. Set the timer to about 12 minutes and set the temperature 180° C/360° F
9. When the timer beeps; turn off your Air Fryer and remove the pan to cool for 5 minutes
10. Serve and enjoy your bacon wraps!

KALE CHIPS

Prep Time: 5 Minutes| Cooking Time: 5 Minutes | Servings: 4

INGREDIENTS:

- 2 tbsp of olive oil
- 4 Cups of loosely packed stemmed kale
- 2 tsp of Ranch Seasoning
- ¼ tsp of salt

DIRECTIONS:

1. Toss the kale chips with the oil
2. Add the ranch seasoning
3. Season the Kale very well with the ranch seasoning and the oil; then place the kale in the basket of your Air Fryer and lock the lid
4. Set the timer to about 4 to 5 minutes and set the temperature to about 370° F
5. Shaking after about 2 minutes; and when the timer beeps; turn off your Air Fryer
6. Serve and enjoy your Kale chips!

AIR FRIED TOMATOES

Prep Time: 5 Minutes| Cooking Time: 5 Minutes | Servings: 4

INGREDIENTS:

- 10 tomatoes, average size
- 1 tbsp of seasoning herbs, basil, dills, oregano, thyme, sage, rosemary or other herbs of your choice.
- 1 pinch of ground black pepper
- 1 tbsp of olive oil

DIRECTIONS:

1. Take the tomatoes in a bowl of convenient size and wash thoroughly. Cut the tomatoes into two pieces in any direction. Turn the pieces over and spray the cooking spray lightly on the whole surface.
2. Turn back the cut halves pieces and spray another cooking spray. Add a pinch of pepper and herbs to taste. For example basil, dills, oregano, thyme, sage, rosemary or other.
3. Put the tomatoes pieces into the basket of the air fryer and set the temperature to 320ºF and cook for 20 minutes. You do not need to preheat it. while it is done of 20 minutes cooking, check with your preferences, Cooking Time: depends on the size of the tomatoes you used and also the number of pieces you slice each tomato.
4. Serve and enjoy your air fried tomatoes!

Chapter 6: Vegetables and Sides

AIR FRIED VEGETABLES

Prep Time: 10 Minutes| Cooking Time: 35 Minutes | Servings: 4

INGREDIENTS:

- 1 and 1/3 cup of Parsnips
- 1 1/3 cup of celery
- 2 Red onions
- 1 ½ cups of Butternut squash
- 1 Tablespoons of olive oil
- 1 Pinch of pepper
- 1 Pinch of salt

DIRECTIONS:

1. Set the temperature of the air fryer to 390oF and preheat it. Clean and peel the onion and also the parsnips. Take onto a cutting board and cut the parsnips into small cubes of 2 cm and chopped the onion. Take the butternut squash, halve it and remove the seeds from the butternut squash no need of peeling it just cut into small cubes.
2. Take the vegetables into a mixture bowl. Add the olive oil and thyme and mix well. Season with the pepper and salt to taste.
3. Now just take the cooking basket from the air fryer and pour the vegetable mixture into it and set the timer of the air fryer to 20 minutes. Cook the item until the timer beep. While the vegetables are nicely brown in color you are done. For the perfect cooking, stir the vegetable after 10 minutes while roasting.

AIR FRIED POTATO BAKE

Prep Time: 10 Minutes| Cooking Time: 25 Minutes | Servings: 4-5

INGREDIENTS:

- 6 medium size, peeled potatoes
- ½ cup of Milk
- ½ Cup of cream cheese
- 1 Teaspoon of black pepper
- ½ Teaspoon of Nutmeg
- ½ Cup of grated cheese, grated

DIRECTIONS:

1. For preheating, set the temperature to 390oF. Take the peeled potatoes on a cutting board and sliced up into thin waters.
2. In a large bowl pour the milk and cream together and mix well. Also add the salt, nutmeg and pepper to taste.
3. Now, take the potato slices and coat with the cream mixture and place them into a heat resistance baking dish. When the potato slices are arranged, pour the milk mixture in the baking dish top of the potato slices.
4. To start baking, take the dish into the cooking basket and start. Cook for 25 minutes. Now, remove the dish from the cooking basket and pour the cheese evenly over the item. Replace the arrangement into the cooking basket and cook for approximately 10 minutes for making it brown in color.

JALAPENO WRAPS WITH BACON

Prep Time: 8 Minutes| Cooking Time: 16 Minutes | Servings: 4

INGREDIENTS

- 13 jalapeno peppers
- 8 ounces room temperature or slightly soft cream cheese
- ½ Cup of crumbled cheddar cheese
- 1 tablespoon of garlic powder
- 1 quarter of teaspoon onion powder
- 13 finely sliced bacon slices
- 1 pinch of salt and 1 pinch of ground black pepper to taste

DIRECTIONS:

1. Cut the jalapenos in half and remove the stems, seeds, and membranes. The more membrane you leave on the jalapenos, the hotter they will be.
2. In a mixing bowl, combine cream cheese, shredded cheddar cheese, garlic powder, onion powder, salt, and pepper. To blend, mix everything together.
3. Fill each jalapeño to the top with the cream mixture using a tiny spoon.
4. Preheat the air fryer to 350°F for about 3 minutes.
5. Cut each bacon slice in half
6. Wrap one slice of bacon around each jalapeño half.
7. Put the bacon-wrapped stuffed jalapenos in a uniform layer in the air fryer, making sure they don't touch.
8. Air fried for 14-16 minutes at 350°F, or until bacon is completely cooked
9. Serve immediately or store in the refrigerator for up to 3 days, warming before serving.

BREADSTICKS

Prep Time: 6 Minutes| Cooking Time: 7 Minutes | Servings: 5

INGREDIENTS:

- 4 Pieces of sliced bread
- 2 Tablespoons of soft butter
- 2 Large eggs
- 1 Pinch of salt: 1 pinch
- Cinnamon, nutmeg, ground cloves and a little icing sugar or maple syrup for serving.

DIRECTIONS

1. Heat the air fryer to 320°F.
2. Take a medium size bowl and break the eggs into it. Gently beaten. Add a pinch of salt, some amount of cinnamon and little cloves and nutmeg. Beat well.
3. Take the bread, cut it into suitable strips and butter both sides.
4. Now, take the strips into the egg mixture and dredge both sides smoothly. And arrange into the basket of the air fryer.
5. Cook it for 2 to 3 minutes. Here, pause the cooking, remove the pan and place it on a heat protected surface. Take a cooking spray and spray it over the bread. When it is done for one side, flip and spray again.
6. Take back it into the fryer and cook for 5 minutes. Check the toast in an interval of 2 minutes. Making sure that the toast frying evenly without burning.
7. When it became golden brown in color, remove the toast from the fryer and serve hot.

AIR FRIED CARROTS

Prep Time: 8 Minutes| Cooking Time: 30 Minutes | Servings: 6

INGREDIENTS:

- 1 Pound of carrots
- 1 Tablespoon of Herbs de Provence, or any herbs of your choice
- 2 Tablespoons of olive oil
- Orange juice: 4 tbsp. or 60ml.

DIRECTIONS:

1. Take a bowl, put the carrots into it and wash it thoroughly. Cut the carrots into chunks. No need to peel the carrots.
2. Now, put the carrots into the pan of the air fryer. Here add the herbs onto the carrot chunks. Quickly pour the oil on the top of the carrots surface so that it can mix with the herbs. It prevents the ingredients from browning.
3. Just roast the item for 20 to 25 minutes. Slowly pour the orange juice into the pan and roast it again for 5 minutes.
4. Serve and enjoy your carrots!

AIR FRIED ACORN SQUASH

Prep Time: 10 Minutes| Cooking Time: 25 Minutes | Servings: 4

INGREDIENTS

- 1 acorn squash, whole
- 1 tbsp olive oil
- 12 tsp kosher salt
- 1 pinch of ground black pepper
- 2 tbsp unsweetened butter (optional)

DIRECTIONS:

1. Preheat the air fryer to 350 degrees Fahrenheit. Wash and dry the acorn squash before cutting it in half lengthwise with a sharp knife. Remove the seeds by scooping them out with the help of a spoon; then discard them.
2. Brush the cut sides with olive oil, then season to taste with salt and pepper. Place the two squash halves, cut side down, in the air fryer basket.
3. Air fry for 15 minutes; then flip the squash carefully so that the sliced sides are facing up.
4. Brush with 1 tablespoon of butter in each cavity, then air fry at 400°F for 5-10 minutes more, or until the squash flesh is golden and fork tender.
5. Serve and enjoy!

AIR FRIED PIZZA

Prep Time: 10 Minutes| Cooking Time: 25 Minutes | Servings: 4

INGREDIENTS:

- Buffalo mozzarella cheese
- 1 pizza dough 12 inches
- 1 tbsp of olive oil
- 1 cup of tomato sauce
- For the toppings (optional)
- 1 tbsp of fresh basilic
- 1 cup of parmesan cheese
- Chilli flakes, to taste

DIRECTIONS:

1. Preheat the air fryer to 190°C (375°F).
2. Spray air fryer basket well with oil.
3. Pat the mozzarella cheese dry with a paper towel to prevent the pizza from getting wet.
4. Roll out pizza dough the same size as the fryer basket. Carefully transfer to fryer, then brush lightly with 1 Tbsp. teaspoon (or more) of olive oil.

5. Spread a light layer of tomato sauce on the dough and sprinkle with mozzarella buffalo cheese.
6. Bake for about 7 minutes, or until the crust is crispy and the cheese has melted
7. Let your pizza cool; then serve and enjoy; you can garnish with basil, grated Parmesan and chili flakes
8. Enjoy your pizza!

ASIAN-STYLE VEGETABLE SPRING ROLLS

Prep Time: 10 Minutes| Cooking Time: 10 Minutes | Servings: 4

INGREDIENTS

- 1 packet of rice paper
- 1 tbsp of cornstarch
- ½ pound of chopped Chinese cabbage
- 1 carrot
- 1 tbsp sesame oil
- 1 cup of bamboo
- 2 spring onions
- 2 cloves of garlic
- 1 tbsp fresh ginger
- 1 tbsp soy sauce
- 1 tbsp of mirin soup

DIRECTIONS:

1. Sauté the garlic and ginger with the oil then add the vegetables, then the soy sauce and vinegar.
2. Mix cornstarch and a little cold water to form a paste.
3. Take each rice paper on a flat surface, add the filling, fold and seal with the cornstarch mixture.
4. Cook for 5 minutes on each side in your Air Fryer basket at 400°F with a little cooking oil, turning them from time to time.
5. Serve and enjoy your spring rolls!

AIR FRIED CHICKPEAS

Prep Time: 10 Minutes| Cooking Time: 15 Minutes | Servings: 4

INGREDIENTS

- 1 can of 1 pound chickpeas
- 1 tbsp olive oil
- ½ tsp paprika
- ½ tsp cumin
- ½ tsp salt and pepper

DIRECTIONS:

1. Drain and rinse the chickpeas. Pat your chickpeas dry with the use of a paper towel or with a clean tea towel.
2. In a bowl mix the olive oil and spices.
3. Add the chickpeas and mix well so that each chickpea is well coated.
4. Pour the chickpeas into the Air Fryer basket and bake for 10 minutes at 200° then remove the basket, sauté the chickpeas and bake for an additional 5 minutes, checking for doneness. They should be toasty and crispy but not hard or burnt.
5. Serve and enjoy your air fried chickpeas!

AIR FRIED POTATO BUNS

Prep Time: 10 Minutes| Cooking Time: 15 Minutes | Servings: 4-6

INGREDIENTS

- 2 cups rising flour (or 120 g plain flour + 2 tsp baking powder)
- 1 ½ pounds sweet potato

DIRECTIONS:

1. Wash and peel the sweet potatoes before chopping them into pieces. Steam them and mash them with a fork or a potato masher.

2. Combine the baking flour and mashed sweet potato in a large mixing dish. At this time, you can add spices to taste.
3. Flour a board lightly and knead the dough for a few minutes.
4. Make a ball, divide it into six equal halves, and then make six little balls. Allow to stand for 1 hour. Optional: Brush the buns with olive oil and top with your favorite garnish or herbs, in this case you can use poppy seeds.
5. Lightly oil the basket and bake for 15 minutes at 350°F.
6. Plate and enjoy your side dish!

AIR FRIED POTATO FRITTERS

Prep Time: 10 Minutes| Cooking Time: 10 Minutes | Servings: 4

INGREDIENTS

- 1 pound sweet potato (raw)
- 1 ½ cups of flour
- 1 garlic clove
- 1 green onion
- 2 tbsp of cajun spices
- 1 tbsp of olive oil

DIRECTIONS:

1. Wash and peel the sweet potato before grating it into a bowl.
2. Finely chop the garlic and onion.
3. Add the flour, the minced garlic, and the spices to the bowl and mix well until a ball is formed. Divide into 6 balls of equal size.
4. Oil a baking tray that fits your Air fryer basket or place the balls and flatten with a spatula to form the patties on a greased baking sheet; then place in the Air Fryer basket
5. Cook at a temperature of 350°F about 5 minutes on each side. You should be able to flip the patties easily.

6. Serve hot or cold!

AIR FRIED POTATOES AND BEETS

Prep Time: 10 Minutes| Cooking Time: 10 Minutes | Servings: 4

INGREDIENTS

- 4 medium potatoes
- 4 beets
- 1 tbsp olive oil
- 1 tbsp Italian seasoning mix

DIRECTIONS:

1. Wash the potatoes well and the beets as well, if possible with a vegetable brush and cut them into cubes of equal size.
2. Place the potato and the beet cubes in a salad bowl and pour in the olive oil and then the seasoning mix. Mix well so that each cube is soaked in the oil spice mixture.
3. Air fry for 20 minutes in the Air Fryer at 350°F
4. Halfway through cooking, take out the basket and shake it.
5. Serve and enjoy your Potatoes and beets!

AIR FRIED MUSHROOMS WITH TERIYAKI SAUCE

Prep Time: 10 Minutes| Cooking Time: 8 Minutes | Servings: 4

INGREDIENTS

- 1 ½ pounds of mushrooms
- 2 tbsp teriyaki sauce

DIRECTIONS:

1. Wash the mushrooms and cut them into not too thin slices because the mushrooms will shrink during cooking.
2. Place the mushrooms in a bowl, pour the teriyaki sauce and mix well.
3. Place the mushrooms in your air fryer basket and cook for 8 minutes at 375°F, making sure to check occasionally for doneness (Cooking Time: may vary depending on Air Fryer model, here we are using the classic Air fryer so there won't be any problem using it).
4. Serve and enjoy your dish!

AIR FRIED CASHEWS WITH PAPRIKA

Prep Time: 6 Minutes| Cooking Time: 15 Minutes | Servings:: 4

INGREDIENTS

- 4 cups cashews
- 2 tbsp olive oil
- 1 tbsp paprika
- 1 tbsp cumin
- 1 tbsp ground coriander
- 1 tbsp salt and pepper

DIRECTIONS:

1. In a bowl mix the olive oil and spices.
2. Add the cashews and mix very well so that the nuts are well soaked.
3. Cooking
4. Pour the walnuts into your Air Fryer basket and bake for about 10 minutes at 360°F then remove the basket
5. Sauté the walnuts or you can also turn them with tongs and Air Fry for an additional 5 minutes, checking for doneness. They should be Air fried to perfection and be crispy but not hard or burnt.
6. For baking, bake for 15 minutes at 200°C on a baking sheet lined with parchment paper!

AIR FRIED FARRO SALAD

Prep Time: 5 Minutes| Cooking Time: 10 Minutes | Servings: 4

INGREDIENTS

- ⅓ cup of orange juice
- 2 tablespoons of red wine vinegar
- 2 tablespoons of chopped walnuts, toasted
- 2 teaspoons of maple syrup
- 2 teaspoons of Dijon mustard
- 1 pinch of sea salt and 1 pinch of freshly ground black pepper , to taste
- 2 medium red beets, peeled and cut into ⅛-inch-thick slices
- 6 cups of fresh baby spinach
- 3 cups of chilled cooked farro (or brown rice)
- 2 fresh pears, cored and chopped
- ¼ cup of onion chopped, red

DIRECTIONS:

1. For the vinaigrette, place the first five ingredients (up to the mustard) in a small blender. Blend until smooth. Season with salt and pepper
2. Preheat air fryer to 350°F. In medium bowl, combine beets with 2 Tbsp. orange mixture. Arrange the beets in the air fryer, overlapping them slightly. Air fry for about 20 minutes or until evenly browned. (Beets may not be crisp). Transfer the beets to paper towel and let rest for 10 minutes. (Beets will be crispy as they cool.)
3. Meanwhile, in a large bowl, combine the spinach, farro (or brown rice), pears and

onion. Drizzle with remaining dressing; toss to coat.
4. Add the beet chips on top.

AIR FRIED CRISPY TOFU WITH CORNSTARCH SALAD

Prep Time: 5 Minutes| Cooking Time: 10 Minutes | Servings: 4

INGREDIENTS

For the crispy air fryer tofu

- 1 package 1 pound (1 lb) firm tofu, broken into bite-sized pieces
- 3 tbsp cornstarch
- 1 tbsp vegetable oil

For the korean sauce

- 2 cloves of garlic, finely chopped
- 3 tbsp ketchup
- 2 tbsp low-salt soy sauce
- 2 tbsp ginger, grated
- 2 tbsp sesame oil
- 1 tbsp gochujang paste or Korean gochujang chili paste.

DIRECTIONS:

1. Preheat your air fryer to 200°C (390°F).
2. In a large bowl, toss the tofu with the oil and coat well. Add cornstarch. Pepper generously and salt lightly.
3. Spray air fryer basket with cooking spray. Place the tofu in the basket, without the pieces touching. Cook 8 minutes, stirring halfway through cooking.
4. Add the Korean sauce and coat the tofu pieces well. Continue cooking until golden and crispy. Serve with rice and cucumber pickles, similar to the original baked recipe.

TOFU AND LETTUCE SALAD

Prep Time: 5 Minutes| Cooking Time: 10 Minutes | Servings: 4

INGREDIENTS

- 1 block of 1 pound
- Tofu marinated in zaatar
- 1 Lemon
- 2 tbsp olive oil
- 1 pinch of salt
- 1 pinch of ground black pepper; to taste
- 1 large head of whole Romaine lettuce or 2 hearts
- 3 cucumbers
- 4 or 5 Radishes
- 2 cups cherry tomatoes
- ¼ cup of fresh mint
- 1 tsp ground sumac

DIRECTIONS:

1. Preheat your Air Fryer to 400°F. Place the pitas in your Air Fryer Basket and Air Fry for about 8 to 10 minutes or until golden brown and dry. Let them cool down and break them into pieces the size of a crouton.
2. Meanwhile, in a large non-stick skillet preheated over medium-high heat, without adding fat, place the marinated tofu and reduce the heat to medium-low. Air fry for 15 to 20 minutes or until golden brown, stirring occasionally.
3. Directly over a salad bowl, squeeze the lemon. Pour in the oil, pepper generously and add a pinch of salt.
4. Coarsely chop the lettuce. Thinly slice the cucumbers and radishes. Cut the cherry tomatoes in half.
5. Add the vegetables to the salad bowl and toss to coat them well with the vinaigrette.
6. Roughly chop the mint.
7. Place the fried tofu on the salad

8. Scoop sesame seeds and herbs from the bottom of the pan to sprinkle over the salad
9. Garnish with mint, toasted pita pieces and sprinkle with sumac. Serve and enjoy your salad!

AIR FRIED BELL PEPPER SALAD

Prep Time: 8 Minutes| Cooking Time: 10 Minutes | Servings: 4

INGREDIENTS

- ¼ pound of red bell peppers
- ½ pound of green bell peppers
- 1 tbsp of lemon juice
- 3 tbsp of yoghurt
- 2 tbsp of olive oil
- ¼ tsp of ground black pepper
- 1 Medium romaine lettuce
- 1 bay leaf

DIRECTIONS:

1. Preheat your Air Fryer to a temperature of about 200°C/400° F
2. Put the bell pepper in the Air Fryer basket and lock the lid of the Air Fryer
3. Set the timer to about 10 minutes and set the temperature to 200° C/400° F
4. When the timer beeps; transfer the peppers to a large plastic bowl and lock it with a plastic wrap
5. Set the peppers aside for 10 minutes
6. Cut the peppers into 4 parts and remove the skin and the seeds
7. Slice the peppers into strips
8. Mix the peppers with a the lemon juice, the yogurt and the olive oil
9. Season with the salt and the pepper
10. Toss bay leaf with the lettuce and garnish the bell pepper strips with it
11. Serve and enjoy your salad!

AIR FRIED VEGETABLES SALAD

Prep Time: 5 Minutes| Cooking Time: 20 Minutes | Servings: 4

INGREDIENTS

- 1 ½ pounds of celeriac
- 2 red onions
- 1 pound of butternut squash
- 1 tablespoon of thyme leaves
- 1 ½ tablespoons of olive oil
- 1 pinch of salt and pepper
- 1 pound of parsnips

DIRECTIONS:

1. Set your Air Fryer's temperature to 400°F.
2. Peel the onions, parsnips, and celeriac. Cut the onions into bits and the parsnips and celeriac into 1 inch cubes. Cut the butternut squash in half, then into cubes after coring it (no need to peel).
3. Combine the thyme and olive oil with the chopped veggies. Season with salt and pepper
4. After adding the veggies, insert the basket into the Air Fryer. The veggies should be roasted for 20 minutes, or until the timer beeps and they are tender and golden brown. During cooking, the veggies were stirred once.
5. After removing the air fryer, season with salt, pepper, and olive oil
6. Serve and enjoy your salad!

AIR FRIED BEET AND CARROTS VEGGIE SALAD

Prep Time: 15 Minutes| Cooking Time: 5 Minutes | Servings: 4

INGREDIENTS:

- 2 cups of cucumber

- 1 head of lettuce
- 1 cup of corn, drained from its water
- 1 cup of roasted pine nuts
- ½ pound of cooked beets
- ½ pound of cooked carrots
- 1 ½ tbsp of rice Vinegar
- 2 tbsp of grated Parmesan
- 1 Pinch of salt
- ¼ tsp of ground black pepper
- 2 tbsp of olive oil

DIRECTIONS:

1. Start by spraying your Air Fryer pan with half the quantity of olive oil
2. Put the carrots and the beets in your Air Fryer basket and drizzle with oil
3. Lock your Air Fryer basket and set the timer to about 5 minutes and set the temperature to 390° F
4. When the timer beeps; turn off your Air Fryer and transfer the beets and the carrots aside to a large bowl
5. Chop the cucumber and the lettuce; then add it to the bowl with the beets and carrots; add in the corn and the rest of your ingredients
6. Shake your salad and mix it with the vinegar, seasoning of salt and pepper
7. Serve and enjoy your salad!

AIR FRIED BACON AND SWEET POTATO SALAD

Prep Time: 10 Minutes| Cooking Time: 25 Minutes | Servings: 4

INGREDIENTS

- 1 ½ pounds sweet potatoes, halved if the potato is large
- 1 tablespoon olive oil
- 1 tbsp flaked sea salt
- 3 slices of smoked bacon cut into ½ inch pieces
- 2 stalks of celery celery, cut into ½ inch slices
- 3 tbsp mayonnaise
- 1 cup of sour cream
- 2 teaspoons white vinegar

DIRECTIONS:

1. Preheat your Air Fryer by selecting AIR FRY, set the temperature to 360°F and the duration to 3 minutes. Select the button START/STOP to begin.
2. Toss the potatoes with oil, salt and pepper as needed in the Air Fryer basket
3. Once the Air Fryer is preheated, add the potatoes to the pan.
4. Air fry at a temperature of about 360°F and time to 25 minutes
5. Select START/STOP to begin
6. After 10 minutes, remove the pan, add the bacon to the potatoes and shake it generously to combine the ingredients. Put the pan back in place to resume cooking.
7. After 20 minutes, remove the pan and check that the potatoes are cooked. If desired, cook for up to 5 more minutes to crisp the potatoes.
8. When cooking is complete, remove your Air Fryer basket
9. Add the potatoes to a large bowl with the remaining ingredients.
10. Mix well and serve hot

AIR FRIED ASPRAGUS SALAD

Prep Time: 10 Minutes| Cooking Time: 25 Minutes | Servings: 4

INGREDIENTS:

- 1 and ½ pounds of trimmed and cut fresh asparagus
- 2 yellow peppers, cut and cubed
- ¼ cup of almonds, toasted.

- ½ cup of grated cheese of Parmesan.
- ½ cup of olive oil
- 3 tbsp of Dijon mustard
- 2 cloves of garlic
- 2 minced teaspoons of lime juice
- 2 teaspoons of sugar
- 1 teaspoon of hot sauce

DIRECTIONS:

1. Preheat your air fryer to 390° F
2. Arrange your asparagus in the basket if the air fryer
3. Mist the asparagus and the bell peppers with ¼ cup of olive oil.
4. Air fry your ingredients for 10 minutes in the preheated air fryer basket
5. Don't forget to shake from time to time to avoid burning.
6. Remove the asparagus from the heat.
7. When it cools, toss the ingredients all together.
8. Add the peppers, the onion, the almond slices and the Parmesan cheese.
9. In another bowl, mix ½ cup of oil, the mustard, the garlic, the lime juice and the sugar.
10. Add the hot sauce and the sauce of the seasoning of the salad.
11. Garnish your salad and serve it. Enjoy!

AIR FRIED EGG AND AVOCADO SALAD

Prep Time: 10 Minutes| Cooking Time: 7 Minutes | Servings: 4

INGREDIENTS:

- 6 lightly cooked eggs
- 2 peeled and chopped avocados
- 1 and ½ cup of chopped tomatoes
- ½ cup of cut of red onion
- A pinch of salt

- A pinch of ground black pepper.
- and ground black pepper
- 2 tbsp of mayonnaise
- 2 tbsp of sour cream
- 1 tbsp of lemon juice
- 9 drops of hot sauce

DIRECTIONS:

1. In the basket of the air fryer, place the thinly sliced eggs.
2. Add the tomatoes, the red onion, the salt, and the pepper all together in a big bowl.
3. Set the timer to 7 minutes.
4. Set the heat to 340°F
5. Turn off the heat, and place the ingredients in a bowl.
6. Stir in your mayonnaise
7. Add the sour cream, the lemon juice, and the hot sauce into the mixture of the mixed egg.
8. Make sure the mixture is evenly coated.
9. Garnish with the avocado.
10. Serve your salad and enjoy its delicious taste!

AIR FRIED PEAR SALAD

Prep Time: 10 Minutes| Cooking Time: 25 Minutes | Servings: 4

INGREDIENTS:

- 1 head of leaf of lettuce that is torn in pieces
- 3 large peeled and cored pears
- ½ cup of Roquefort cheese
- 1 crumbled and peeled avocado
- ½ pitted, diced and peeled cup of sliced onion.
- ¼ cup of white sugar
- ½ cup of pecans
- 1/3 cup of olive oil
- 3 tbsp of red wine
- 1 and ½ teaspoon of white sugar.
- 1 and ½ teaspoons of mustard

- 1 clove of minced garlic
- ½ teaspoon of salt

DIRECTIONS:

1. In a preheated air fryer and over a medium heat, stir in ¼ cup of white sugar
2. Add the pecans.
3. Set the timer to 5 minutes and the heat to 340° F.
4. Keep stirring until the sugar gets melted and the pecans become caramelized.
5. Transfer the nuts on waxed papers.
6. Let it cool and break it into small pieces.
7. Place the cooked ingredients in a mixing bowl and mix very well
8. For the dressing, add the oil, the vinegar
9. Add 1 and ½ teaspoon of sugar
10. Add the mustard
11. Add the chopped garlic
12. Add the salt, and the pepper.
13. In a huge serving bowl
14. Arrange the lettuce, the pears, the blue cheese, the avocado, and the green onions.
15. Pour the dressing over the salad
16. Sprinkle the salad with the pecans, and serve it!

AIR FRIED BACON AND SWEET POTATO SALAD

Prep Time: 10 Minutes| Cooking Time: 25 Minutes | Servings: 4

INGREDIENTS:

- 1¼ to 1½ pounds of radishes with their tops
- 2 tbsp of olive oil
- 1 teaspoon of salt
- ½ teaspoon of ground black pepper
- ½ pound of fresh and sliced mozzarella into half moons shape.
- 2tbsp of glaze, balsamic oil

DIRECTIONS:

1. Start by washing the radishes very well under cold and running water.
2. Rinse it very well and pat dry your radish using towel papers.
3. Make sure to rim wilted stems from the radish.
4. In a large bowl, put the radish and drizzle it with oil, a pinch of salt and a pinch of pepper.
5. Toss the ingredients all together very well until they are combined.
6. In the basket of the air fryer, place the ingredients.
7. Set the heat to 350° F and the timer to 35 minutes.
8. Lock the lid of the air fryer and let your components bake
9. Once your timer goes off, start by removing your radish from your Air Fryer
10. Arrange everything on a platter together with the mozzarella.
11. Pour a little bit of oil on the radish and serve it.
12. Enjoy the breathtaking taste of your salad.

AIR FRIED POTATOES AND PARSNIPS SALAD

Prep Time: 10 Minutes| Cooking Time: 35 Minutes | Servings: 4

INGREDIENTS:

- 4 Washed, peeled and sliced potatoes into thin rounds
- 3 Peeled and very thinly- sliced parsnips
- 4 tablespoons of olive oil
- ½ Teaspoon of salt
- ¼ Teaspoon of black pepper
- 1 Finely cut leek
- 2 Minced garlic cloves

- 1/3 Cup of maple syrup
- 2 Tablespoons of Dijon mustard
- 2 Tablespoons of fresh parsley

DIRECTIONS

1. Preheat your air fryer to about 390° F
2. Put the sliced sweet potatoes with the parsnips into a large bowl and add to it about 2 tablespoons of olive oil to it
3. Season your ingredients with a little bit of salt and ground pepper; then toss the ingredients very well
4. Arrange the sliced pieces of the potatoes and parsnips into a baking tray and drizzle with oil
5. Pour the oil in top of the ingredients and add the garlic with the leeks
6. Stir in the maple syrup and the Dijon
7. Put the baking pan in the air fryer basket and close the lid
8. Set the timer to about 35 minutes and the temperature to about 375° F
9. When the timer beeps, remove the baking pan from the air fryer
10. Serve and enjoy.

AIR FRIED CAESAR SALAD

Prep Time: 12 Minutes | Cooking Time: 15 Minutes | Servings: 4

INGREDIENTS:

- 4 handfuls of green salad, batavia or lettuce, washed and drained
- 2 large eggs
- 1 Wholemeal Bread
- 1 clove of garlic
- 2 chicken fillet (about 1 pound)
- 2 tomatoes
- 1 cup of parmesan

Light Caesar sauce:

- 1 natural yoghurt; 1 ½ cups
- 1 tbsp of capers to taste
- 1 small tsp of mustard
- 1 tbsp of cider or wine vinegar
- 2 tbsp of olive oil
- 1 cup of chives
- 1 pinch of salt
- 1 pinch of ground black pepper

DIRECTIONS:

1. Cook the eggs until they are hard, 10 minutes in boiling water. At the end of this time, put in very cold water to stop the cooking and thus cool them.
2. Spray your Air fryer basket with cooking spray and cook the chicken fillet in the Air Fryer basket for 10 minutes over a temperature of 400°F
3. Check the cooking by inserting a knife in the heart, if the juice comes out pink; continue cooking.
4. Season with salt, pepper and leave to rest
5. Meanwhile, prepare the Caesar sauce, mix the mustard with the oil and vinegar; add the yoghurt then the gherkins (or capers) previously chopped with a knife and the chives.
6. Taste and season with salt and pepper if necessary
7. Place the sliced bread in your Air Fryer basket and scrape over the peeled garlic clove from both sides of the bread.
8. Air fry for 5 minutes, then remove the bread from the air fryer and cut into cubes.
9. Wash and cut the tomatoes and hard-boiled eggs into quarters. Cut the chicken into thin slices.
10. On the plates, place the green salad, then the tomatoes, chicken and hard-boiled eggs, pour the Caesar sauce; add the garlic bread and parmesan
11. Serve and enjoy your salad!

Chapter 7: Poultry Mains Recipes

AIR FRIED CHICKEN BREASTS

Prep Time: 11 Minutes | Cooking Time: 15 Minutes | Servings: 4

INGREDIENTS

- 3 Boneless and Skinless Chicken Breasts
- 2 tablespoons of softened grass fed Salted Butter
- 1 teaspoon of dried Italian Seasoning
- 1/2 teaspoon of Smoked paprika
- 1 Pinch of salt and Pepper to taste

DIRECTIONS:

1. Start by placing the chicken breasts over a cutting board with the help of a sharp knife; then cut each of the breasts into half lengthwise to have by the end 4 chicken portions.
2. Combine the seasonings in a small bowl with the butter; then spread the prepared mixture over the top of each of the chicken cutlets
3. Place the chicken cutlets in your air fryer and cook at a temperature of about 370°F for about 10 to 15 minutes and make sure to check after about 10 minutes; you can use an internal meat thermometer; the temperature of the meat should be 165°F
4. Remove the chicken from the air fryer
5. Serve and enjoy your dish!

AIR FRIED TURKEY TENDERS

Prep Time: 10 Minutes | Cooking Time: 10 Minutes | Servings: 4

INGREDIENTS

- 10 turkey tenders
- 1 ¼ Cups of Crushed pork rinds
- 1 teaspoon of Salt
- 1 teaspoon of Smoked paprika
- ½ teaspoon of Garlic powder
- ½ teaspoon of Onion powder
- 2 large Beaten Eggs

DIRECTIONS

1. In a medium shallow bowl, combine the crushed pork rinds with the prepared seasonings; then in a separate shallow bowl, place in the beaten eggs and coat the chicken tenders into the egg; then into the mixture of the pork
2. Put the turkey tenders in your air fryer and set your air fryer to a temperature of about 400°F for about 10 minutes; then flip half way through
3. Serve your delicious dish!

AIR FRIED TANDOORI CHICKEN

Prep Time: 10 Minutes | Cooking Time: 11 Minutes | Servings: 4

INGREDIENTS

- 1 Pound of diced chicken
- ½ Finely chopped small cabbage
- 2 Grated carrots
- ½ Teaspoon of ground turmeric
- ½ Teaspoon of chili powder
- ½ Teaspoon of ground coriander
- ½ Teaspoon of ground cumin
- ½ Teaspoon of Masala powder
- ½ Teaspoon of salt
- 1 handful of chopped fresh coriander
- 5 Tablespoons of all purpose flour

DIRECTIONS:

1. Combine altogether the chicken, the cabbage and the carrots. Season the chicken with the turmeric, the chili powder, the ground coriander, the cumin, the Masala, the salt and the fresh coriander.
2. Add the flour to water and make a kind of heavy mixture
3. Mix your ingredients very well
4. Preheat your air fryer to about 350° F
5. Arrange the chicken in the basket steamer of the air fryer
6. Close the lid of your air fryer and set the timer to about 11 minutes
7. When the timer beeps, remove the chicken from the air fryer, then serve and enjoy it!

AIR FRIED CHEESE CHICKEN WINGS

Prep Time: 10 Minutes | Cooking Time: 30 Minutes | Servings: 4-6

INGREDIENTS

- 2 Pounds of raw wings and chicken drums
- 2 teaspoons of garlic powder
- 2 teaspoons of onion powder
- 2 teaspoons of smoked paprika
- 1 pinch of sea salt and 1 pinch of cracked pepper
- 1 and ½ tablespoons of cornstarch or tapioca powder

For the sauce:

- 3 tablespoons of butter
- 1 teaspoon of onion powder
- 2 teaspoons of garlic powder
- 1 pinch of cracked black pepper
- ½ cup of grated parmesan (split into half)
- 8 celery stalks, chopped into about 16 pieces

DIRECTIONS:

1. Set your air-fryer to a temperature of about 400F.
2. Pat the wings dry with a clean paper towel; then place them in a large bowl.
3. Add in the seasonings and thoroughly rub the cornstarch all over the chicken wings
4. Place the chicken wings into the air fryer basket and air-fry the chicken wings for about 25 to 30 minutes; then flip halfway and once you finish; add to a clean and large mixing bowl
5. Place a large skillet over a medium high heat; then add in the butter and sprinkle in the parmesan and stir
6. Remove from the heat: then pour the butter on top of the chicken wings
7. Garnish with dried parsley and black pepper
8. To prepare the ranch; add your ingredients to a large mixing bowl or a blender and mix very well until it becomes smooth
9. Serve and enjoy your dish!

CHICKEN NUGGETS WITH MAYONNAISE

Prep Time: 10 Minutes | Cooking Time: 25 Minutes | Servings: 4

INGREDIENTS:

- 3 Medium breasts of Chicken
- ¼ Cup of Mayonnaise
- 1 Teaspoon of white vinegar
- 1 Cup of All purpose flour
- ½ Teaspoon of sea salt
- ¼ Teaspoon of black pepper
- 2 Tablespoons of olive oil

DIRECTIONS:

1. Fill in a deep and large bowl with the water and add to it a little bit of salt

2. Put the chicken into the salty water and set it aside to brine for about 15 minutes
3. Drain the chicken and pat it dry with paper towels
4. Cut the chicken meat into the size of nuggets
5. In a medium bowl, whisk altogether the vinegar and the mayonnaise. In a separate bowl, combine the all purpose flour and a little bit of salt; then add a dash of black pepper
6. Coat the chicken pieces with the mayonnaise and press it into the mixture of the all purpose flour
7. Preheat your air fryer to around 350° F
8. Arrange the chicken nuggets in the basket of the air fryer and drizzle with a little bit of oil; then close the lid
9. Set the timer to about 8 minutes
10. When the timer beeps; remove the chicken from the air fryer; then serve and enjoy your snack!

BURRITO CHICKEN

Prep Time: 10 Minutes| Cooking Time: 10 Minutes | Servings: 4-5

INGREDIENTS:

- 3 Large eggs
- 2 Chicken breasts; cut into slices
- 1/3 red bell Pepper
- ¼ sliced Avocado
- 1/6 cup of grated Mozzarella cheese
- 2 tbsp of salsa
- 1 pinch of salt and pepper
- Tortilla, as needed

DIRECTIONS:

1. Take a convenient size bowl and break the eggs into it. Add a pinch of salt and pepper to taste.
2. Now, in a non-stick pan pour the eggs mixture and takes it to the basket of air fryer. Set the temperature to 360°F and cook for 5 minutes.
3. Remove the basket from the air fryer and carefully separate the eggs to a bowl.
4. Now, fill your tortilla, cut the chicken breast, avocado, salsa and red pepper and fill with the eggs.
5. Use tin foil to line up the air fryer and place the burrito onto it. Set the time to 300°F and cook for 3 minutes.
6. Serve and enjoy your dish!

AIR FRIED PAPRIKA CHICKEN

Prep Time: 8 Minutes| Cooking Time: 15 Minutes | Servings: 4-6

INGREDIENTS

- 3 Boneless and Skinless Chicken Breasts
- 2 tablespoons of softened grass fed Salted Butter
- 1 teaspoon of dried Italian Seasoning
- 1/2 teaspoon of Smoked paprika
- 1 Pinch of salt and Pepper to taste

DIRECTIONS:

1. Start by placing the chicken breasts over a cutting board with the help of a sharp knife; then cut each of the breasts into half lengthwise to have by the end 4 chicken portions.
2. Combine the seasonings in a small bowl with the butter; then spread the prepared mixture over the top of each of the chicken cutlets
3. Place the chicken cutlets in your air fryer and cook at a temperature of about 370°F for about 10 to 15 minutes and make sure to check after about 10 minutes; you can use an internal meat thermometer; the temperature of the meat should be 165°F
4. Remove the chicken from your air fryer
5. Serve and enjoy your dish!

AIR FRIED CHEDDAR CHICKEN MUFFINS

Prep Time: 8 Minutes| Cooking Time: 30 Minutes | Servings: 4

INGREDIENTS:

- 1 Skinless and boneless chicken breast
- 2 Large Eggs
- ½ Cup of chopped Celery
- ¼ Cup of chopped Red Onion
- ½ Teaspoon of Lemon
- 1 Pinch of pepper
- 2 Tablespoons of Bacon Bits
- ¼ Cup of fat Free Cheddar Cheese
- 1 Teaspoon of Crushed Red Pepper
- ½ Teaspoon of Garlic Powder
- ¼ Teaspoon of Salt

DIRECTIONS:

1. Drain the chicken and chop it into very small pieces Chop the Celery and the Red Onions.
2. Mix all of the ingredients into a bowl very well. Grease a muffin pan with cooking spray and distribute the batter into the small ramekins
3. Preheat your air fryer to about 350° F and put the ramekins in the basket of your air fryer and close the lid
4. Set the timer to about 30 minutes and the temperature to about 355 ° F
5. When the timer beeps, remove the pan from the air fryer and let the chicken muffins cool for about 5 minutes
6. Serve and enjoy your chicken muffins!

AIR FRIED WHOLE CHICKEN

Prep Time: 10 Minutes| Cooking Time: 30 Minutes | Servings: 4-6

INGREDIENTS

- A whole chicken of 3 ½ pounds
- 1 tablespoon of olive oil
- 1 tbsp of chicken seasoning
- 1 teaspoon of kosher salt or to taste
- ½ teaspoon of paprika
- ½ teaspoon of garlic powder
- ¼ teaspoon of black pepper
- ⅙ teaspoon of dried thyme leaves

DIRECTIONS:

1. Make sure the chicken's cavity is empty and pat the skin dry very well
2. Now, apply the olive oil to the skin before seasoning it.
3. Put your chicken breast-side down in the basket of your air fryer. Untie the legs if necessary, or press it to flatten it a little till it fits if your chicken is too big (and touches the top element).
4. Set your air fryer to 350 degrees. , make sure your air fryer can fit your chicken before putting it in
5. Cook the chicken for 20 to 30 minutes after turning it over, or until an instant-read thermometer registers 165°F.
6. Take out the chicken of the air fryer, let sit for ten minutes
7. Cook vegetables in the air fry by pouring the chicken drippings over them (such as green beans, asparagus, or cauliflower).
8. Serve and enjoy your whole chicken!

AIR FRIED CHICKEN CHOPS WITH CASHEWS

Prep Time: 10 Minutes| Cooking Time: 30 Minutes | Servings: 4

INGREDIENTS

- 2 Cups of cashew nuts
- 1 Teaspoon of olive oil
- 1 Teaspoon of coriander powder
- 1 Teaspoon of red chili powder

- ½ Teaspoon of Garam Masala powder
- ½ Teaspoon of black pepper powder
- 1 Teaspoon of Black salt
- ½ Teaspoon of salt
- 2 Teaspoons of fry mango powder
- 1 whole chicken

DIRECTIONS

1. Chop the chicken into small pieces
2. Combine all of your ingredients into a large mixing bowl and mix it very well
3. Line your ingredients into the steamer basket of your air fryer and combine it very well
4. Set your air Fryer to a temperature of about 340 degrees Fahrenheit
5. When the timer beeps, remove the chicken from the air fryer and let it rest for about 10 minutes
6. Serve and enjoy your chicken with cashews!

AIR FRIED CHICKEN WITH BROCCOLI

Prep Time: 10 Minutes | Cooking Time: 30 Minutes | Servings: 2-4

INGREDIENTS

- 1 ½ Pounds of chopped into medium bites of chicken breasts; 2 to 3
- 1 Cup of broccoli florets (frozen or fresh)
- 1 Chopped zucchini
- 1 Cup of bell chopped pepper
- ½ Chopped Onions
- 2 Minced or crushed garlic cloves
- 2 tablespoons of olive oil
- ½ teaspoon of garlic powder, salt, chili powder, and pepper
- 1 tablespoon of Italian seasoning (or of spice blend of your choice)

DIRECTIONS:

1. Preheat your air fryer to a temperature of about 400°F.
2. Chop your veggies and the chicken into bites of small size; then transfer to a large mixing bowl
3. Add the oil and the seasoning to the large bowl and toss very well to combine
4. Add in the chicken and the veggies to the preheated air fryer and cook for about 10 minutes
5. If your air fryer is small; you can cook into 2 to 3 batches
6. Serve and enjoy your chicken!

AIR FRIED BUFFALO CHICKEN WITH BLUE CHEESE

Prep Time: 6 Minutes | Cooking Time: 30 Minutes | Servings: 4

INGREDIENTS:

- ½ Teaspoon of garlic powder
- ½ Teaspoon of paprika
- ½ Teaspoon of chili powder
- 1/8 Teaspoon of black pepper
- ½ Tablespoon of olive oil
- 8 Chicken Strips tenderloin of about 12 oz
- ¼ Cup of Hot Sauce
- 4 Trimmed celery stalks
- ½ Cup of skinny blue cheese

DIRECTIONS:

1. Preheat your air fryer to a degree of 350° F
2. Combine the garlic powder, the paprika, the chili powder and the black pepper into a medium deep bowl.
3. Season the chicken with the spices and toss it very well
4. Arrange the chicken in the basket of your air fryer and close the lid

5. Set the timer to about 10 minutes and the temperature to around 350° F
6. When the timer beeps, remove the chicken from the air fryer; then transfer it to a serving dish
7. Pour the sauce over your chicken
8. Serve and enjoy your delicious dish!

AIR FRIED CHICKEN BITES

Prep Time: 10 Minutes| Cooking Time: 15 Minutes | Servings: 6

INGREDIENTS:

- 1 ½ Pounds of ground chicken
- ½ Cup of yellow onion, diced
- ¼ Cup of diced red bell pepper
- 2 Tablespoons of minced fresh mint
- 2 Tablespoons of red curry paste
- 1 Teaspoon of ground cumin
- 1 and ½ teaspoon of minced fresh ginger
- ½ Teaspoon of ground coriander
- ½ Teaspoon of sea salt
- ¼ Teaspoon of black pepper

DIRECTIONS:

1. Preheat your air fryer to about 350°F and grease a baking tray that fits your air fryer basket
2. Mix all of your ingredients into a bowl and shape it into about 15 meatballs
3. Arrange the meatballs in the basket of your Air fryer
4. Close the lid of the air fryer and set the timer to about 15 minutes and the temperature to about 350° F
5. When the timer beeps, remove the meat balls from the air fryer
6. Serve and enjoy your mouth-watering taste chicken bites!

CHICKEN SPINACH NEST

Prep Time: 10 Minutes| Cooking Time: 10 Minutes | Servings: 4

INGREDIENTS

- 4 large Potatoes
- 1 Teaspoon of salt
- ½ Pound of shredded or finely cut cooked chicken
- ½ Teaspoon of pepper
- 2 and ½ teaspoon of garlic powder
- 2 and ½ teaspoons of onion powder
- 4 Teaspoons of vegetable oil
- 2 Tablespoons of cooking spray
- 4 Cups of thawed spinach thawed
- 4 Tablespoons of extra virgin olive oil
- 4 Beaten eggs

DIRECTIONS:

1. Preheat your air fryer to about 390° F
2. Start by grating the potatoes; then add 1 pinch of salt and combine the ingredients very well; then set it aside into a colander and put a bowl under the colander for about 15 minutes
3. Into a large non-stick skillet; sauté the shredded chicken and the spinach into 1 tablespoon of olive oil
4. Season with 2 teaspoons of garlic powder and 2 teaspoons of onion powder
5. Add a little bit of salt and sauté for about 4 minutes and when it is done, set it aside
6. Season your ingredients with ½ teaspoon of garlic powder and ½ teaspoon of onion powder
7. Add ½ teaspoon of pepper and pour in 4 teaspoons of vegetable oil; then mix very well.
8. Spray a 9 muffin tin pan with a little bit of cooking spray.

9. Arrange the grated potatoes into the muffin cups and press it into the bottom.
10. In a small and deep bowl, mix the eggs with a little bit of salt; then add the spinach and the shredded chicken
11. Put the potatoes in each of the nests
12. Place your baking tin in the basket of the air fryer and close the lid
13. Set the timer for about 15 minutes and the heat to 350° F.
14. When the timer beeps, remove the muffin tin from the air fryer and set it aside for about 10 minutes to cool down
15. Remove from the oven and let them cool slightly.
16. Serve and enjoy!

AIR FRIED CHICKEN THIGHS

Prep Time: 10 Minutes| Cooking Time: 15 Minutes | Servings: 4

INGREDIENTS

- 2 Pounds of boneless and skinless chicken thighs
- 1 tsp of turmeric powder
- 1 tsp of coriander powder
- ½ tsp of white pepper
- ½ tsp of cumin powder
- 1 cup of cream cheese
- 1 tsp of fish sauce
- 2 tsp of grated ginger
- 2 tbsp of hot sauce
- Avocado oil cooking spray

DIRECTIONS:

1. In a large mixing bowl, place the turkey things with the ingredients from the turmeric to the hot sauce; then gently combine and cover your bowl
2. Store in the refrigerator for about 30 minutes or
3. Lightly spray your air fryer basket with the avocado oil; then drip off the marinade and put the chicken thighs into the air fryer basket in one layer making sure to leave a distance between each of the pieces
4. Air fry at a temperature of about 370°F for about 8 minutes on the first side; then for about 8 to 10 minutes on the second side
5. Serve hot and enjoy your mesmerizing dish!

AIR FRIED CHICKEN WINGS

Prep Time: 7 Minutes| Cooking Time: 25 Minutes | Servings: 4

INGREDIENTS

- 10 Chicken Wings
- ¾ Cup of Potato Starch
- ¼ Cup of Clover Honey
- 1/4 cup of butter
- 2 Tablespoons of Fresh minced Garlic
- ½ Teaspoon of Kosher Salt

DIRECTIONS:

1. Start by rinsing and drying your chicken wings
2. Put the potato starch in a large bowl and coat the chicken wings with it
3. Arrange the chicken wings in the basket of your air fryer and close the lid
4. Set the timer to about 25 minutes and the temperature to 375° F
5. Make sure to shake the basket of the air fryer each 4 to 5 minutes.
6. When the timer beeps; remove the chicken wings from the air fryer
7. Put a medium pot over the stove and set the heat to low
8. Add the butter to the pot and add the garlic
9. Sauté the crushed garlic for about 4 minutes
10. Add the honey and the salt and let simmer for around 22 minutes; make sure to stir from time to time

11. Arrange the chicken wings in a serving platter and pour the honey sauce over it
12. Serve and enjoy your delicious dish!

AIR FRIED CHINESE STYLE CHICKEN

Prep Time: 7 Minutes | Cooking Time: 10 Minutes | Servings: 4

INGREDIENTS:

- 1 Pound of diced chicken meat
- 1 and ½ tablespoons of corn flour
- 1 Large beaten egg
- 1 and ½ tablespoons of all-purpose flour
- 1 pinch of salt
- 1 Pinch of ground black pepper
- 2 Tablespoons of cooking oil
- 2 Tablespoons of crushed ginger
- 2 Tablespoons of crushed garlic
- 2 Tablespoons of crushed green chili pepper
- 2 Tablespoons of chopped cilantro
- 1 Cup of chicken stock
- 1 Tablespoon of soya sauce
- ¼ Teaspoon of salt
- ¼ Teaspoon of ground black pepper
- ¼ Teaspoon of sugar

DIRECTIONS:

1. Mix the corn flour, the flour, the salt and the pepper with the lightly beaten egg to make your batter.
2. Dip the pieces of chicken into your batter and arrange the pieces in the basket of the air fryer
3. Close the lid and set the timer to about 10 minutes and the temperature to 340° F. In the mean time; prepare the Chinese sauce by heating the oil into a saucepan and sautéing the garlic and the ginger to it
4. Add the green chilies and the cilantro leaves; then fry altogether for about 1 minute.
5. Reduce the heat and add chicken stock, the soya sauce, the salt, the sugar, the pepper and cook for 6 additional minutes.
6. Add the mixture of corn flour with the water and let boil.
7. Add the air fried chicken and cook it for about 2 minutes.
8. Serve and enjoy hot!

AIR FRIED STUFFED CHICKEN

Prep Time: 10 Minutes | Cooking Time: 30 Minutes | Servings: 3

INGREDIENTS:

- 4 Boneless, pounded and skinless chicken breasts
- 14 Oz of diced tomatoes
- ¼ Cup of pesto
- 6 slices of sliced Provolone Cheese
- 1 Cup of Italian style bread crumbs

DIRECTIONS:

1. Preheat your air fryer to about 390° F.
2. Lay the pounded chicken on a cutting surface and toss 1 tablespoon of pesto over each of the chicken pieces
3. Put pieces of cheese on top of the pesto
4. Spoon about 1 tablespoon of the canned tomatoes and roll the chicken; then secure it with a tooth pick
5. Pour the remaining quantity of tomatoes right into the bottom of your baking tray.
6. Roll the pieces of the chicken through the breadcrumbs.
7. Arrange the chicken into the tomatoes and spray the chicken with a non-stick spray.
8. Put the baking pan in the basket of the air fryer and close the lid
9. Set the timer for about 30 minutes and the temperature for about 375° F

10. When the timer beeps, remove the chicken from the heat; then serve and enjoy your chicken dish without any delay!

CHICKEN STUFFED MACARONI WITH CASHEWS

Prep Time: 10 Minutes| Cooking Time: 15 Minutes | Servings: 4

INGREDIENTS:

- 10 Oz of large macaroni shells
- 1 Pound of minced cooked chicken
- ½ Diced white onion
- 4 Minced garlic cloves
- 1 Cup of soaked raw cashews
- 1 and ½ cups of vegetable broth
- 1 Tablespoon of cornstarch
- ½ Teaspoon of cumin
- ¾ Teaspoon of chilli powder
- 2 Tablespoons of nutritional yeast
- 1 Can of 4 oz cut chill
- 1 Cup of tortilla chips
- 1 Cup of cilantro for garnishing

DIRECTIONS:

1. Start by crushing the tortilla chips into very fine pieces of crumbs; then put the crumbs in a baking pan lined with a parchment paper
2. Pour olive oil on the bread and sprinkle with a little bit of salt and pepper
3. Put the baking pan in the basket of the air fryer and close the lid
4. Set the timer to about 10 minutes and the temperature to about 350° F; in the mean time; boil the macaroni according to the instructions on the package; then in a medium wok and over a low heat, sauté the onion with the chicken and with the garlic and a drizzle of olive oil in a non-stick wok; then set the ingredients aside
5. Add the onions and the garlic to a food processor with the rest of the ingredients except for the tortilla and add just ½ of the peppers
6. Drain your noodles and set it aside and cover it
7. Add the cheese of cashew and cook the mixture until it becomes consistent
8. Add your macaroni with the rest of the green chillies and stir very well
9. Put the ingredients together in a baking tray and add the tortilla chips and the cilantro
10. Put the tray of the macaroni in the basket of the air fryer and close the lid
11. Set the timer to about 5 minutes and the temperature to about 350°F
12. When the timer beeps, serve and enjoy!

STUFFED JUMBO SHELLS

Prep Time: 10 Minutes| Cooking Time: 15 Minutes | Servings: 4

INGREDIENTS

- 1 Head of cauliflower, cut into small florets
- 2 Tablespoons of extra-virgin olive oil
- ¼ Cup of nutritional yeast
- ½ Cup of unsweetened milk
- 2 Teaspoons of garlic powder
- 1 Teaspoon of onion powder
- ½ Bunch of finely chopped fresh parsley leaves
- 1 teaspoon of sea salt
- 12 Oz jar of tomato sauce
- 1 Package of 12 Oz cooked jumbo shells

DIRECTIONS

1. Preheat your air fryer to about 390° F
2. Put the cauliflower in a blender with the olive oil, the nutritional yeast, the milk, the garlic powder, the onion powder, the parsley, and the sea salt.

3. In a baking tray that fits your air fryer; spread the sauce of tomato; then stuff the pasta shells with the mixture of the cauliflower and season very well with salt and ground pepper
4. Arrange the jumbo shells in the baking tray and stir in the remaining quantity of the tomato sauce
5. Put the tray in the air fryer basket and set the timer to about 15 minutes and the temperature to about 390° F
6. When the timer beeps, remove the tray from the air fryer; then top with fresh basil leaves
7. Serve and enjoy your dish!

AIR FRIED CRISPY CHICKEN

Prep Time: 10 Minutes| Cooking Time: 30 Minutes | Servings: 4-6

INGREDIENTS :

- 1 and a half cups buttermilk (milk buttermilk)
- 1/4 cup hot sauce (Red Hot style)
- 1 tablespoon paprika
- 1 tablespoon onion powder
- 1 tbsp garlic powder
- 1 tablespoon of salt
- 1 tbsp pepper
- 2 to 3 pound chicken pieces (drumstick, thigh)
- 1 and a half cups flour
- 1/2 cup cornstarch
- 1 teaspoon baking powder
- 1 tbsp of olive oil (Vegetable, Avocado, Canola)

DIRECTIONS :

1. In a small bowl, combine paprika, onion powder, garlic powder, and salt and pepper.
2. Make brine with the buttermilk, hot sauce and half the spice blend.
3. Add chicken and brine to a large zip lock bag and soak for 1-2 hours or overnight.
4. In a plastic bag, add flour, cornstarch, baking powder and remaining spices. Shake well to mix.
5. Add three chicken pieces at a time to the bag and shake well to coat the chicken pieces. Transfer the chicken pieces to a bowl. Repeat with all the chicken pieces.
6. Dip the floured chicken pieces back into the bag of brine.
7. Return the chicken pieces to the flour bag one last time and shake.
8. Let sit for 10 minutes while you preheat your air fryer to 350°F (175°C).
9. Spray the chicken pieces and the bottom of the fryer with oil.
10. Cook for 15 minutes on one side. Flip, spray other side with oil and cook another 15 minutes or until thermometer insert reads 165°F in white meat and 175°F in dark meat.

AIR FRIED CHICKEN BAKE

Prep Time: 10 Minutes| Cooking Time: 15 Minutes | Servings: 4

INGREDIENTS:

- 2 or 3 large eggs
- ½ of sliced chorizo sausage
- 1 Big cubed potato
- 1 Cup of cooked and shredded chicken meat
- ½ Cup of frozen corn
- 2 Tbsp of olive oil
- 2Tbsp of finely chopped parsley
- 1 feta wheel
- 1 Pinch of pepper and 1 pinch of salt

DIRECTIONS:

1. Grease a baking tray that fits your air fryer with butter
2. Boil the potatoes in a medium pan over a medium heat for about 15 minutes

3. In the baking pan, pout the potato, the chorizo and the corn.
4. Set your air fryer at a temperature of about 350° F and bake in the sausage and the shredded chicken meat
5. Once your ingredients are cooked, pour your ingredients in the baking pan and add to it the eggs and the potatoes.
6. Season very well with salt and pepper
7. Pour the eggs over your ingredients in the baking pan and top it with the crumbled feta; then sprinkle with parsley and put the baking tray in the basket of the air fryer
8. Sprinkle with finely chopped parsley and cook for about 10 minutes in your air fryer
9. Once the timer beeps; remove from your feta from the air fryer; then serve and enjoy it hot

AIR FRIED CHICKEN AND SWEET POTATO

Prep Time: 10 Minutes| Cooking Time: 22 Minutes | Servings: 4

INGREDIENTS:

- 2 Minced garlic cloves
- ½ Cup of diced onion
- 1 Diced red pepper
- 2 Stripped and cut bacon
- 1 Pound of diced chicken
- 1 Spiralized sweet potato
- 2 Cups of spinach
- ½ Cup of water or broth
- 1 Teaspoon of paprika
- ½ Teaspoon of Cayenne
- 1 Teaspoon of salt-free all-purpose seasoning
- 6 Beaten eggs

DIRECTIONS:

1. Preheat your air fryer to about 350° Fahrenheit

2. In a deep and large pan, sauté the garlic, the onion, the peppers, the bacon, the chicken and the sweet potato until the chicken is cooked very well
3. Add the spinach, the water and the seasonings; then cook for about 5 minutes
4. Transfer your mixture to a baking pan that fits your air fryer basket; meanwhile, combine the eggs in a deep bowl and pour it over your mixture
5. Put the baking tray in the basket of your air fryer and close the lid
6. Set the timer to about 20 minutes and the temperature to about 370°F

AIR FRIED SPINACH STUFFED CHICKEN

Prep Time: 10 Minutes| Cooking Time: 22 Minutes | Servings: 4

INGREDIENTS:

- 3 to 4 chicken breasts
- 8 Oz of chopped frozen cooked spinach
- ½ Cup of crumbled feta
- 4 Oz of cream cheese
- 1 Diced garlic clove
- ¼ Teaspoon of divided salt
- ⅛ Teaspoon of pepper
- 1 tablespoon of olive oil

DIRECTIONS:

1. Preheat your air fryer to about 390° Fahrenheit
2. Combine the frozen and chopped spinach, the feta, the cream cheese, the garlic and half of the quantity of salt into a deep bowl.
3. Make a small pocket into each of the chicken breast with the knife
4. Divide the cheese and the spinach into about three parts; then roll it into logs
5. Stuff each of the logs into the chicken pocket you have made into the chicken breast

6. Season the chicken with the pepper and the salt
7. Grease a baking tray that fits your Air Fryer and put the chicken in the tray
8. Put the chicken in the basket of the air fryer and set the timer for about 15 minutes and the temperature to 350° Fahrenheit
9. When the timer beeps, remove the chicken from the air fryer; then serve and enjoy your chicken dish!

AIR FRIED CHICKEN AND SWEET POTATOES

Prep Time: 10 Minutes | Cooking Time: 15 Minutes | Servings: 4

INGREDIENTS

- 2 pounds chicken breasts cut into strips
- 1 Tsp of salt, divided
- ½ tsp ground black pepper, divided
- 2 large eggs
- ½ cup buttermilk
- ¼ cup Red-hot Hot Sauce, divided
- ½ cup all-purpose flour
- 3 tbsp vegetable oil
- 2 tbsp brown sugar
- 1 tsp of chili powder
- ½ tsp of garlic powder
- ½ tsp of paprika
- 1 cup dill pickle slices

DIRECTIONS:

1. Preheat air fryer to 400°F (200°C). Season the chicken strips with ½ tsp salt and ¼ tsp. pepper. In a bowl, whisk the eggs, buttermilk and 2 Tbsp. Tbsp hot sauce. In another bowl, mix the flour and the rest of the salt and pepper.
2. Dip the chicken strips in the egg mixture; drain them, before rolling them in the flour.
3. Arrange the chicken strips on a well-greased deep fryer baking sheet and cook for 12 to 15 minutes, flipping halfway through cooking, until cooked through, browned and crispy.
4. In a large bowl, whisk together the oil, brown sugar, chili powder, garlic powder, paprika and remaining hot sauce, then add the chicken strips, stirring to coat them completely and evenly with the mixture .
5. Serve with sliced dill pickles.

Note: Before you begin, clean all countertops and wash your hands with soap and warm water. Also remember to wash utensils and cutting boards as well as your hands after any contact with raw meat or eggs. Avoid cross-contamination by using a different plank for meat and other foods. Be sure to cook your food to safe temperatures and refrigerate leftovers within two hours. For more food safety tips, visit our home food safety section.

Chapter 8: Beef Recipes

AIR FRIED BEEF RELLENOS

Prep Time: 12 Minutes | Cooking Time: 25 Minutes | Servings: 4

INGREDIENTS:

- 1 Pound of ground beef
- 2 Cans of green chilies
- Oz of cream cheese
- 1 tsp of cumin
- 1 tsp of paprika
- 1 tsp of chili powder
- 1 tsp of garlic powder
- 1 Pinch salt
- 1 pinch black pepper
- 1 tsp of dried minced onion
- 1 Beef bouillon cube
- Mexican shredded cheese
- Chopped cilantro

DIRECTIONS:

1. Preheat your Air Fryer to a temperature of about 375° F for about 5 minutes
2. Start by browning the beef in a skillet and drain it very well off any grease
3. Add the dry seasonings with a little of water, the water and the beef cube and let the mixture simmer for about 5 minutes
4. Slice the chilies into a lengthwise way; then spoon about 1 tbsp of the cream cheese in each of the green chilies and place it in your Air Fryer pan
5. Add the mixture of the meat to the pan and place the pan in your Air Fryer
6. Lock the lid and; set the temperature to about 390° F and set the timer to about 20 minutes
7. When the timer beeps; turn off your Air Fryer and sprinkle the cheese then cook for about 5 minutes

AIR FRIED BEEF MEATLOAF

Prep Time: 10 Minutes | Cooking Time: 16 Minutes | Servings: 4

INGREDIENTS:

- 1 pound of ground beef
- 2 eggs
- 1 Cup of diced onion
- ¼ Cup of chopped cilantro
- 1 tbsp of minced ginger
- 1 tbsp of minced garlic
- 2 tsp of Garam Masala
- 1 tsp of salt
- 1 tsp of turmeric
- 1 tsp of cayenne
- ½ tsp of ground cinnamon
- 1/8 tsp of ground of cardamom

DIRECTIONS:

1. In a large mixing bowl, combine all the ingredients together
2. Form a meat loaf from your meat mixture
3. Place the meatloaf in your Air Fryer pan
4. Place the pan in your Air Fryer and lock the lid
5. Set the timer to about 16 minutes and set the temperature of 365°F
6. When the timer beeps; turn off your Air Fryer; then set the meatloaf aside to cool for 5 minutes
7. Slice your Meatloaf; then serve and enjoy its delicious taste!

AIR FRIED BEEF MEATBALLS

Prep Time: 10 Minutes | Cooking Time: 10 Minutes | Servings: 4-5

INGREDIENTS:

- 1 small onion
- 1 ½ pounds of ground beef
- 1 cup of chopped parsley
- ½ tbsp. finely chopped thyme leaves
- 1 large Egg
- 1 cup of breadcrumbs.
- 1 pinch of pepper
- 1 Pinch of salt
- 9 Oz of tomato sauce

DIRECTIONS:

1. Peel the onion and take it onto the cutting board. Finely chopped. Take a large bowl and place the beef, parsley, thyme leaves, egg, and breadcrumbs together and mix well. Add the salt and pepper to taste. From the mixture make ten to twelve meatballs.
2. Set the temperature of the air fryer to 390°F and preheat. Take the basket from the air fryer and arrange the meatballs into a heat resistant woven dish add the tomato sauce and place the dish into the air fryer basket.
3. Now cooking set the temperature to 330°F and the timer to 5 minutes. Cook for 5 minutes.
4. Serve and enjoy your meatballs!

AIR FRIED BEEF AND SALAD

Prep Time: 10 Minutes | Cooking Time: 40 Minutes | Servings: 4

INGREDIENTS:

- 3lb topside of beef meat
- tbsp of olive oil
- 1pinch of salt
- 1pindh of black pepper
- For the salad: Take 2 grated carrots, ½ medium grated white cabbage, 1 finely sliced red pepper, 1 pinch of sugar snap peas, 1 pinch of bean sprouts and 1tbsp of toasted sesame seeds with 1 small bunch of coriander leaves that are chopped (remember to keep some aside for garnish)
- For dressing your dish: 2 tbsp of fish sauce+ 2 tbsp of fresh lime juice+ 2 red chillies+ 2 cloves of garlic+ 1 pinch of ginger powder + 2 tbsp of tamari or soy sauce+ 2 tbsp of sesame oil
- 4 tbsp of water
- 1 tbsp of brown sugar.
- chopped shallots
- 1 Pinch of salt

DIRECTIONS:

1. Preheat the air fryer to its maximum temperature for 3 minutes.
2. Meanwhile, prepare your beef meat.
3. Rub the beef with oil, the salt and the pepper.
4. Roast the beef meat in the air fryer basket for around 30 minutes, then turn the temperature to 380° F for around 10 minutes
5. Meanwhile, prepare your salad by mixing all the ingredients together and leave it aside.
6. Now place the ingredients in a food blender and blitz it for 1 minute.
7. Drizzle some of the dressing over the salad.
8. Once the meat is perfectly roasted, remove it and set it aside for 20 minutes.
9. Cut the meat into slices and serve it with the salad.
10. Garnish your meat with coriander, peanuts and you can also add lime wedges.
11. Enjoy an amazing dish!

BEEF FAJITAS

Prep Time: 10 Minutes | Cooking Time: 35 Minutes | Servings: 5

INGREDIENTS:

- 2 pound of beef that is cut into thin strips
- 6 tbsp of vegetable oil
- ½ cup of lemon or lime juice
- 4 peeled and mashed garlic cloves
- ½ teaspoon of chilli powder
- 1 seeded and sliced red pepper
- 1 yellow seeded and sliced pepper
- 2 medium thinly sliced onions
- 2 tbsp of olive oil
- 12 tortillas
- 2 tbsp of melted butter
- Use amasai for topping
- 1 Avocado

DIRECTIONS:

1. Prepare a combination of oil and lemon or lime juice
2. Add the spices and mix the ingredients very well with beef meat.
3. Marinate for 5 hours.
4. Remove the marinated mixture from the fridge and pat dry the meat.
5. Take the basket of the air fryer and arrange the meat portions in it.
6. Pour 2 tbsp of olive oil over the meat.
7. Set the timer to 35 minutes.
8. Set the heat at 360° F
9. In the meantime, sauté the vegetables in the vegetable oil and after that add it to your air fryer basket.
10. Heat the tortillas for a short time in a non stick pan and brush it with the melted butter.
11. Serve your beef meat with the tortillas and enjoy it!

BEEF WITH HERBS

Prep Time: 10 Minutes | Cooking Time: 15 Minutes | Servings: 4

INGREDIENTS

For the herb lemon butter:

- ½ stick of unsalted butter at room temperature
- 3 tbsp of chopped fresh parsley
- 1 tsp of chopped thyme
- ½ tsp of lemon zest
- 1 Pinch of salt
- 1 Pinch of black pepper

For the Steak:

- 2 pounds of beef steak
- 2 tbsp of olive oil

DIRECTIONS:

To make the herb lemon butter:

1. Mix all together the butter with the parsley, the thyme, the lemon zest, the salt and the pepper into a small bowl.
2. Transfer the mixture to a parchment paper and form into a shape of log
3. Roll the butter into the parchment paper to about 1 and ½ inches into diameter making sure to twist the ends and to close and refrigerate

To make the steak:

1. Preheat your air fryer to a temperature of about 400°F / 200°C.
2. Rub the oil on both the sides of the steaks and season with the salt and the black pepper.
3. Add the prepared steaks to the air fryer and cook for about 12 minutes per side making sure to flip the meat halfway through

4. When cooked to doneness; make sure to remove from your air fryer and let rest for about 5 minutes
5. Top with the refrigerated herb butter; then serve and enjoy your dish

BEEF TERIYAKI

Prep Time: 12 Minutes| Cooking Time: 12 Minutes | Servings: 3

INGREDIENTS:

- 2 tablespoons of soy sauce
- Salt and pepper
- beef steaks
- medium-sized potatoes
- 1 cup of snow peas
- 1 tbsp of olive oil
- 21.76 oz mushrooms
- 1 large onion

DIRECTIONS:

1. Cut the beef steaks into strips and place them in a marinade of soy sauce, olive oil, and ketjap. Brush the mushrooms spotless and cut them into quarters. Wash the snow peas and cut the onion into half-rings.
2. Mix every one of the vegetables together with one tablespoon of olive oil.
3. Peel the potatoes and cut a little cut off the base with the goal that they lie level. Make little entry points in the potatoes, yet not the distance to the base. Put some oil between the entry points and sprinkle the potatoes with salt and pepper.
4. Bake the potatoes in the Air fryer for 20 minutes at 390°F
5. At that point, slide the potatoes to the side and place the vegetables and the beef in the center.
6. Cook for about 5 additional minutes

SPICY BEEF STEAK

Prep Time: 15 Minutes| Cooking Time: 15 Minutes | Servings: 3-4

INGREDIENTS:

- 4 Medium garlic cloves
- 1 Pinch of kosher salt
- 1 pound of trimmed and chopped steak
- 1 Pinch of freshly ground black pepper
- 2 tbsp of avocado oil
- 2 Oz of unsalted butter
- 1 tbsp of chopped fresh flat-leaf parsley

DIRECTIONS:

1. Start by peeling the garlic clove and smash it
2. Sprinkle a little bit of garlic and 1 pinch of salt and 1 pinch of ground black pepper
3. Clean the steak and pat it dry with a clean paper towel
4. Spray your Air Fryer with cooking spray; then add the steak the garlic
5. Add the garlic and the butter; then rub it very well over the steak
6. Place the baking pan in you Air Fryer and set the timer to 15 minutes and the temperature to about 350° F
7. When the timer beeps; turn off your Air Fryer
8. Slice the steak and garnish it with parsley
9. Serve and enjoy your dish!

BEEF MIGNON WITH HERBS

Prep Time: 10 Minutes| Cooking Time: 12 Minutes | Servings: 4

INGREDIENTS:

- 3 beef Mignons filets
- 2 Teaspoons of coarse salt
- 1 and ½ teaspoons of freshly ground black pepper
- 1 Teaspoon of olive oil

- 1/8 teaspoon of cayenne pepper
- 2 Oz of crumbled blue cheese
- 1 Tablespoon of divided butter
- 1 and ½ teaspoons of cannabis infused butter
- 2 Teaspoons of finely chopped fresh chives

DIRECTIONS:

1. Season the steaks of beef on the two sides with a little bit of salt and 1 pinch of ground pepper
2. Preheat your air fryer to about 375° F
3. Grease a baking tray with cooking spray; then add the steaks and drizzle it with a little bit of vegetable oil
4. Add the butter and put the baking tray in the basket of the air fryer; then close the lid
5. Set the timer to 6 minutes and the temperature to about 350°F
6. When the timer beeps, remove the steaks from the air fryer and pour the melted butter on top of the steaks; then sprinkle with cheese
7. Serve and enjoy your dish!

AIR FRIED BEEF BURGERS

Prep Time: 15 Minutes| Cooking Time: 20 Minutes | Servings: 4

INGREDIENTS

- 1 Pound of Mixed Mince beef
- 1 Onion
- 1 tsp of Garlic Puree
- 1 tbsp of Tomato Puree
- 1 tsp of Mustard
- 1 tsp of Basil
- 1 tsp of Mixed Herbs
- 1 Pinch of salt
- 1 Pepper
- 1 cup grated Cheddar Cheese
- Cabbage leaves, as needed

DIRECTIONS:

1. Mix the beef mince with the seasoning and combine it very well
2. Form the beef mince into burgers of medium size; then place it in the Air Fryer pan and lock the lid
3. Set the timer to about 25 minutes and the temperature to about 200° C/400° F
4. When the timer beeps, open your Air Fryer and flip the burgers; then return the pan to the Air Fryer and cook for about 20 more minutes
5. When the timer beeps; turn off your Air Fryer
6. Transfer the burgers to a serving platter
7. Place 1 cabbage leaf in the bottom
8. Place the burger over the cabbage leaf; then add another layer of cabbage leaf
9. Serve and enjoy your burgers!

AIR FRYER GREEK STYLE BEEF CHOPS

Prep Time: 15 Minutes| Cooking Time: 15 Minutes | Servings: 4

INGREDIENTS

- 7 to 8 trimmed beef chops
- 3 Crushed garlic cloves
- 1 teaspoon of extra-virgin olive oil
- ½ fresh Lemon
- 1 and ¼ teaspoons of kosher salt
- 1 tbsp of Za'atar
- 1 Pinch of fresh ground pepper, to taste

DIRECTIONS:

1. Rub the chops of beef with the oil and the garlic
2. Now squeeze the lemon over both the sides of the meat; then season with 1 pinch of salt, the black pepper and the zatar

3. Preheat your air fryer to a temperature of about 400°F
4. Air fry your beef chops in batches in one layer and cook for about 6 to 7 minutes per side
5. Serve and enjoy your dish!

AIR FRIED BEEF WITH VEGGIES

Prep Time: 10 Minutes | Cooking Time: 30 Minutes | Servings: 4

INGREDIENTS

- pounds of thinly sliced Sirloin Steak
- 3 Chopped into 2 to 3 pieces Green Scallions
- 1 Cup of shredded carrots
- 1 Cup of shredded carrots
- 2 tablespoons of splenda
- 2 tablespoons of melted olive oil
- 2 Tablespoons of Sesame Seeds
- 2 teaspoons of Minced Garlic
- 2 teaspoons of Minced Garlic
- ½ teaspoon of Ground Black Pepper
- ½ Teaspoon of Ground Black Pepper

DIRECTIONS:

1. Place the sliced beef, the carrots, and the green onions in a plastic zip-top bag
2. Add the splenda; the olive oil, the sesame seeds, the garlic and the ground pepper; then add the salt
3. Squish the bag very well; then let the beef marinate for about 30 minutes or for about 24 hours in your refrigerator; then place the meat and the veggies into your Air Fryer basket
4. Set your air fryer to a temperature of about 400°F and the timer to 12 minutes
5. Remove the meat from the air fryer; then serve with rice cauliflower or a salad of your choice

AIR FRIED MONGOLIAN BEEF

Prep Time: 10 Minutes | Cooking Time: 20 Minutes | Servings: 4

INGREDIENTS:

- 1 pound of thinly sliced Flat Iron steak against the grain
- ¼ cup of olive oil
- 3 Cut into 1 inch of length and diagonally sliced Green onions

For the Mongolian Beef Marinade:

- 1 teaspoon of peeled and grated Fresh root ginger
- 2 Chopped garlic cloves
- 1 tbsp of sesame

DIRECTIONS:

1. Start to cut the Flat Iron Steak into thin slices against the grain.
2. Place the sliced beef in a small ziplock bag; then add the peeled and grated root ginger and the garlic
3. Let marinate for about 1 hour in the refrigerator
4. When you are ready to cook the meat; drain it very well from the marinade; then reserve the liquid for later use
5. Preheat your Air Fryer for about 5 minutes to a temperature of 375°F
6. Spray your Air Fryer basket with cooking spray; then add the meat to the Air Fryer Basket and cook with the lid closed for about 15 to 20 minutes
7. Remove the meat from your air fryer and sprinkle with the sesame
8. Serve and enjoy your dish!

AIR FRIED SPARE RIBS

Prep Time: 10 Minutes| Cooking Time: 10 Minutes | Servings: 4

INGREDIENTS

- 1 tablespoon of olive oil
- 1 teaspoon of minced Garlic
- 1 teaspoon of minced Ginger
- 1 tablespoon of fermented black bean paste
- 1 tablespoon of Shaoxing Wine
- 1 tablespoon of agave nectar
- 1 ½ pounds of Spare Ribs, chopped into small pieces

DIRECTIONS:

1. In a large mixing bowl, combine all together all your ingredients and let marinate.
2. Add in the spare ribs and mix very well; then let the ribs marinate for about 30 minutes
3. When you're ready to cook your dinner; remove the spare ribs from the marinade; then place in your air fryer basket
4. Set your air at a temperature of about 8 minutes
5. Remove the meat from your Air Fryer
6. Serve and enjoy your dish!

SPICY AIR FRIED STEAK WITH MUSHROOMS

Prep Time: 10 Minutes| Cooking Time: 18 Minutes | Servings: 4

INGREDIENTS

- 1 pound of steaks, chopped into cubes of about ½ inches
- 8 oz of cleaned, washed and halved mushrooms
- 2 Tablespoons of olive oil
- 1 tbsp of Worcestershire sauce (low sodium)
- ½ teaspoon of garlic powder
- 1 Pinch of flaky salt, to taste
- 1 Pinch of fresh cracked black pepper, to taste
- 1 Dash of Finely minced parsley
- Chili Flakes

DIRECTIONS:

1. Rinse and pat dry the steak cubes; then combine the meat and the mushrooms
2. Coat with the melted olive oil and season with the Worcestershire sauce; the garlic powder and a generous seasoning of pepper and salt
3. Preheat your Air Fryer at a temperature of about 400°F for about 4 minutes.
4. Spread the steak and the mushrooms in one even layer in the air fryer basket. Air fry at 400°F for about 10 to 18 minutes making sure to flip and shake from time to time
5. Garnish with chopped parsley and drizzle with chilli flakes
6. Season with additional pepper and salt
7. Serve and enjoy your dish!

AIR FRIED BEEF SATAY

Prep Time: 5 Minutes| Cooking Time: 12 Minutes | Servings: 2-

INGREDIENTS:

- 2-3 tablespoons sweet soy sauce
- 2 tablespoons vegetable oil
- 1 ½ pounds lean beef
- 2 cloves garlic, pounded
- 1 inch crisp ginger root, ground or 1 teaspoon ginger powder
- 2 teaspoons bean stew paste or hot pepper sauce
- 1 teaspoon ground coriander
- 1 shallot, finely slashed
- 1 cup of unsalted peanuts, ground

DIRECTIONS:

1. Mix half of the garlic in a dish with the ginger, 1-teaspoon hot pepper sauce, 1-tablespoon soy sauce, and 1-tablespoon oil. Mix the beef with the mixture and leave to marinate for 15 minutes.

2. Preheat the Air Fryer to 390°F.
3. Put the marinated beef in the basket and slide it into the Air Fryer. Set the clock to 12 minutes and roast the beef until darker and done. Turn once while roasting.
4. In the interim, make the nut sauce: warm 1-tablespoon oil in a pan and delicately sauté the shallot with the rest of the garlic. Include the coriander and sear for a brief timeframe more.
5. Mix the peanuts with 1-teaspoon hot pepper sauce and 1-tablespoon soy sauce with the shallot mixture and tenderly bubble for 5 minutes, while blending. If essential, include a tad bit of water if the sauce gets too thick.
6. Season to taste with soy sauce and hot pepper sauce

AIR FRIED STEAK WITH PESTO

Prep Time: 5 Minutes| Cooking Time: 12 Minutes | Servings: 2-4

INGREDIENTS:

- 2 tablespoons red pesto
- 1 pinch of freshly ground pepper
- 1 tablespoon (hot) paprika powder
- 2 cuts stale white bread, in pieces
- 1 clove garlic, pounded
- 21.76 oz beef, in pieces
- 1 egg yolk + two egg whites

DIREECTIONS;

1. Grind the bread with the paprika powder in the food processor until you have a brittle mixture and mix in the olive oil. Exchange this mixture to a bowl.

2. Then purée the beef filet in the food processor and mix with the egg yolk, garlic, pesto, and parsley. Include ½-teaspoon salt and pepper to taste.

3. Preheat the Air Fryer to 390°F.

4. Whisk the egg whites in a bowl. Shape the beef mixture into 10 balls and press them into oval chunks. Coat the pieces first with egg white and after that with breadcrumbs. The pieces must be covered with scraps everywhere.

5. Put five chunks in the basket and slide it into the Air Fryer. Set the clock to 10 minutes. Sear the chunks brilliant darker. At that point rotisserie the rest of the chunks

AIR FRIED BEEF LIVER

Prep Time: 5 Minutes| Cooking Time: 10 Minutes | Servings: 4

INGREDIENTS

- 8 oz of beef liver
- ¼ cup of flour
- 1 Dash of onion powder sprinkle
- 1 Dash of garlic powder
- ½ cup of milk
- 1 Large egg
- 2 tbsp of olive oil

DIRECTIONS:

1. Remove the beef livers from the container; then rinse and dry over a paper towel; make sure to dry the liver very well
2. Combine the flour and seasonings into a small bowl; then combine the egg and the milk in a medium separate bowl; you should get a bow for the egg and another one for the flour
3. One filled with milk and eggs, and one filled with a flour mixture for coating the chicken livers
4. Dip the livers into the milk mixture; then into the flour mixture; then lay on the Air Fryer pan or basket. Continue the process until it is complete
5. Using olive oil or cooking spray Olive Oil, spray the livers all over and the all purpose flour
6. Air fry for about 8 to 10 minutes

Chapter 9: Lamb Recipes

AIR FRYER MACADAMIA AND ROSEMARY CRUSTED LAMB

Prep Time: 15 Minutes| Cooking Time: 20 Minutes | Servings: 4

INGREDIENTS

- 1 clove of garlic
- 1 tablespoon olive oil
- 2 pounds rack of lamb
- 1 pinch of salt and pepper
- 1 ½ cups unsalted macadamia nuts
- 1 tablespoon breadcrumbs (preferably homemade)
- 1 tablespoon chopped fresh rosemary
- 1 egg

DIRECTIONS:

1. Finely chop the garlic. Mix olive oil and garlic to get garlic oil. Brush the rack of lamb with oil, then season with salt and pepper.
2. Preheat the Air fryer to 200°F.
3. Finely chop the walnuts and place them in a bowl. Add breadcrumbs and rosemary. Beat the egg in another bowl.
4. Dip the meat into the egg mixture, making sure to drain well. Coat the lamb in the macadamia nut crust.
5. Place the coated rack of lamb in the Air fryer basket and slide the basket into the unit. Set the timer for 25 minutes. After 25 minutes, increase the temperature to 400° F and add 5 minutes to the timer. Remove the meat and let it rest, covered with aluminium foil, for 10 minutes before serving.
6. Tip: If you wish, you can replace the macadamia nuts with pistachios, hazelnuts, cashews or almonds.

SPICY LAMB

Prep Time: 30 Minutes| Cooking Time: 20 Minutes | Servings: 4

INGREDIENTS

For the Lamb:

- ½ tablespoons of Ground Cumin
- 1 teaspoon of Sichuan peppers or ½ teaspoon of cayenne
- 1 pound of lamb shoulder; cut into pieces of about ½ inch each
- 2 tablespoons of vegetable oil
- 1 tablespoon of minced garlic
- 2 Chopped red Chili Peppers
- 1 teaspoon of Kosher Salt
- ¼ teaspoon of splenda

For finishing:

- 2 finely chopped Green Scallions
- 1 large handful of chopped cilantro

DIRECTIONS:

1. In a heavy and dry skillet, roast about 2 tablespoons of cumin seeds with the cayenne or the Sichuan red peppers
2. When the skillet cools down; use a pestle and mortar to give a quick grind.
3. Poke the lamb with a fork to make holes into the meat; then in a large bowl; marinate the meat with cumin; Sichuan pepper, oil, red chilli peppers and splenda; then let marinade for about 30 minutes
4. Set your air fryer to a temperature of about 360F for about 10 minutes; then place the marinated lamb in one layer in your Air fryer basket and cook

5. When the timer beeps; mix in the cilantro and the chopped scallions; then serve and enjoy your delicious dish!

LAMB BURGERS

Prep Time: 30 Minutes| Cooking Time: 18 Minutes | Servings: 4

INGREDIENTS:

For the lamb Burgers:

- 1 Pound of minced Lamb
- 2 Teaspoons of Garlic Puree
- 1 Teaspoon of Harissa Paste
- 1 Tablespoon of Moroccan Spice
- 1 Pinch of salt
- 1 Pinch of Pepper
- For the Greek Dip:
- 3 Tablespoons of Greek Yoghurt
- 1 Teaspoon of Moroccan Spice
- ½ Teaspoon of Oregano
- 1 Small lemon, only the juice

DIRECTIONS:

1. In a large mixing bowl; put the lamb burger ingredients in a large bowl and mix very well until everything is seasoned
2. With a burger press; shape the mince into the shape of lamb burgers
3. Put the lamb burgers in your air fryer and cook for about 18 minutes at a temperature of about 180c/360°F.
4. While your ingredients are cooking; make the Greek Dip
5. Remove the meat from the Air Fryer
6. Serve and enjoy your recipe!

CRUSTED LAMB WITH ORANGE

Prep Time: 10 Minutes| Cooking Time: 10 Minutes | Servings: 4

INGREDIENTS:

- 2 racks of lamb
- 1 tbsp of olive oil
- 1 pinch of salt
- 1 pinch of ground black pepper
- 1 cup of fresh leaves of parsley
- 2 minced garlic cloves.
- 1 orange grated zest
- ¾ cup of toasted and finely chopped almonds
- 2 tablespoons of Dijon mustard

DIRECTIONS:

1. Preheat your air fryer to 390°F
2. Rub your lamb using olive oil
3. Season the lamb with salt, olive oil and pepper.
4. Arrange your lamb in the basket of the air fryer.
5. Set the timer to 12 minutes and the heat to 390° F
6. Meanwhile, mix th²e garlic, the parsley, the orange zest and the almonds all in a deep bowl.
7. Remove the racks of the lamb of the air fryer; then spread on each lamb rack 1tbsp of Dijon mustard, herbs and nuts.
8. Divide the mixture between the racks of the lamb evenly
9. Return the lamb to the air fryer and keep cooking for 10 more minutes.
10. Serve and enjoy your dish with salad!

STUFFED FLAT BREAD WITH LAMB

Prep Time: 10 Minutes| Cooking Time: 20 Minutes | Servings: 4

INGREDIENTS:

- 1 ½ pounds of ground lamb
- 2 tbsp of olive oil
- 1 yellow peeled and finely sliced onions
- 2 tbsp of seasoning mix
- 1 cup of washed baby spinach leaves
- ¼ Cup of toasted pine nuts
- 2 tbsp of currants
- 1 pinch of salt and 1 pinch of black pepper
- 2 Flat breads
- 1 cup of crumbled feta
- ½ cup of fresh parsley leaves

DIRECTIONS:

1. Preheat your air fryer to 390°F.
2. Season the lamb with the salt and the black pepper.
3. Form the lamb into balls
4. Drizzle 1tbsp of oil. Place the lamb in the air fryer basket
5. Slide the basket in the air fryer and set the timer to 10 minutes.
6. Air fry your lamb meat for about 10 minutes. Once the lamb is cooked, remove it from the air fryer and place it in a skillet with heated 1tbsp of oil
7. Over a low heat, add your onion and cook, don't forget to keep stirring for 3 minutes until soft and light golden
8. Add the seasoning spices
9. Add your spinach and cook for 2 minutes.
10. Remove the dish from the heat and add the pine nuts with the currants.
11. Season using salt and pepper.
12. Now, cut the bread into halves.
13. Create 2 large flat pieces of bread in order to use it on a baking sheet
14. Top the flat breads with the mixture of the lamb
15. Sprinkle using crumbled feta.
16. Bake the flat breads in the air fryer at a heat of 320° F
17. After 10 minutes, serve and enjoy your delicious dish.

AIR FRIED LAMB RIBS

Prep Time: 9 Minutes| Cooking Time: 10Minutes | Servings: 4

INGREDIENTS

- 1 Rack of lamb rib (about 2 pounds)
- 2 Teaspoons of chopped fresh rosemary
- 1 Teaspoon of chopped fresh thyme
- 2 Minced garlic cloves
- 1 Pinch of Salt
- 1 Pinch of ground black Pepper
- 2 Tablespoons of olive oil

DIRECTIONS:

1. Preheat your air fryer to about 375° F.
2. Prepare the marinade by mixing the rosemary with the thyme and the garlic
3. Sprinkle with a pinch of the ground black pepper
4. Place all of your ingredients in a plastic bag and add the olive oil
5. Set the marinated lamb in the refrigerator for about 30 minutes to 1 hour before air frying it or you can leave it for an entire night.
6. Remove your lamb from the refrigerator and bring it to the room temperature.
7. Arrange the lamb rack in the basket steamer of the air fryer

8. Make a few cuts through the lamb and sprinkle it with a little bit of salt and pepper
9. Close the lid of the Air Fryer and set the timer to 35 to 40 minutes and the temperature to about 390° F
10. When the timer beeps, unplug the air fryer; then serve and enjoy your roasted lamb with salad and lemon wedges.

AIR FRIED LAMB KOFTAS

Prep Time: 10 Minutes| Cooking Time: 15 Minutes | Servings: 4

INGREDIENTS:

- 1 ½ pounds of ground lamb meat
- 1 egg
- 3 tablespoons of breadcrumbs
- 1 large red onion
- 1 teaspoon ground cumin
- 1 teaspoon of paprika powder
- 3 sprigs of fresh coriander
- 3 sprigs of fresh mint
- 1 pinch of salt
- 1 pinch of ground black pepper

DIRECTIONS:

1. Finely chop the red onion or spring onions.
2. Chop the mint and coriander leaves.
3. Mix the ground lamb, beaten egg, the breadcrumbs, the chopped onion, chopped herbs, paprika, cumin, salt and pepper.
4. Form large balls of the mixture and let them rest for 30 minutes to an hour in the fridge.
5. Lengthen each ball by hand before pricking it on iron skewers that fits your Air fryer basket.
6. Heat your Air Fryer for about 5 minutes to 400°F
7. Arrange the koftas in the basket of your Air Fryer and drizzle with olive oil
8. Air Fry for about 8 minutes

9. Once cooked, remove the meat koftas from your Air Fryer
10. Serve and enjoy your koftas!

AIR FRIED LAMB CHOPS WITH HERBS

Prep Time: 10 Minutes| Cooking Time: 9 Minutes | Servings: 4

INGREDIENTS

- 1 head of garlic
- 3 tablespoons of olive oil
- 1 tablespoon fresh oregano, finely chopped
- 1 pinch sea salt
- 1 pinch ground black pepper
- 8 lamb chops

DIRECTIONS:

1. Preheat the air fryer to 400°F. Brush the head of garlic with a thin layer of olive oil and place it in the basket. Insert the basket into the air fryer and set the timer for 12 minutes. Roast the garlic until cooked.
2. Meanwhile, toss the herbs with sea salt, pepper and olive oil. Lightly brush the chops with half a tablespoon of the olive oil/herb mixture and let stand for 5 minutes.
3. Remove the head of garlic from the basket and preheat the air fryer to 400°F.
4. Arrange four lamb chops in the basket and insert it into the air fryer. Set the timer for 9 minutes. Roast the chops until golden brown. They may remain red or pink inside. Keep them warm in a dish and air fry the rest of the chops in the same way.
5. Squeeze the garlic cloves between your thumb and forefinger over the olive oil/herb mixture. Add salt and pepper. Stir the mixture well.
6. Serve the lamb chops with the garlic sauce.
7. Serve and enjoy with braised zucchini

Chapter 10: Pork Recipes

AIR FRIED PORK SAUSAGE

Prep Time: 8 Minutes | Cooking Time: 10 Minutes | Servings: 4

INGREDIENTS

- 1 Pound of Italian sausage
- 1 Peeled and sliced onion
- 1 Sliced green pepper
- 1 Sliced red pepper
- 1 tablespoon of Italian seasoning
- 2 tablespoons of olive oil

DIRECTIONS:

1. In a medium small mixing bowl; combine all together the sliced peppers with the onions, the olive oil and the Italian seasoning
2. Coat your vegetables with olive oil
3. Put the vegetables in your Air Fryer
4. Add the sausages near your vegetables
5. Set the temperature of your Air Fryer to a temperature of about 400°F and the timer to about 10 minutes
6. Plate your dish; then serve and enjoy your dish!

AIR FRIED PORK WITH CHEESE

Prep Time: 10 Minutes | Cooking Time: 18 Minutes | Servings: 4

INGREDIENTS

- 4 Boneless, chopped into portions pork of about ½ inch each
- 1 Pinch of salt and ground black pepper to taste
- 1 Large egg
- ⅓ Cup of grated Parmesan cheese
- ⅓ Cup of flour
- ½ Teaspoon of salt
- ¼ teaspoon of pepper
- ¼ teaspoon of garlic powder
- 2 Tablespoons of avocado oil

DIRECTIONS:

1. Season the pork chops with 1 pinch of salt and 1 pinch of pepper on both the sides of the pork
2. Beat the egg in a medium bowl; then mix the Parmesan cheese with the all purpose flour about ½ teaspoon of salt, ¼ teaspoon of pepper, and the garlic powder all together in a separate bowl
3. Dip each of the pork chops into the egg wash; then into the Parmesan-flour mixture to coat very well
4. Place in your Air Fryer basket and spritz with the avocado oil.
5. Cook into your air fryer at a temperature of about 375°F for about 10 to 12 minutes
6. Flip the pork chops and cook for about 3 to 4 additional minutes
7. Remove the pork from the Air Fryer
8. Serve and enjoy your dish!

AIR FRIED STUFFED PORK CHOPS WITH CHEESE AND KALE

Prep Time: 11 Minutes | Cooking Time: 10 Minutes | Servings: 4

INGREDIENTS

- 8 thick-cut pork chops
- 8 oz of cream cheese
- 1 tbsp of Garlic Powder
- ½ tbsp of dried Rosemary
- ½ tbsp of dried Oregano

- 1 tsp of crushed red pepper
- ½ cup of mozzarella cheese
- 3 tbsp of jalapenos
- 1 cup of kale
- 1 Pinch of salt and 1 pinch of Pepper to Taste

DIRECTIONS:

1. Preheat your air fryer to a temperature of about 390°F degrees.
2. With the help of a sharp knife, cut the pork chops down the center 80% of the way to butterfly it.
3. Season the meat with the salt and the pepper
4. In a separate bowl, add the cream cheese and the desired spices together with the kale.
5. Mix your ingredients very well until your ingredients are very well combined.
6. Take about 1/6th of the filling; then place into the pocket of each of the pork chops; then fold over
7. Put the filling of the pork chops with the side up in your Air Fryer basket
8. Don't over crowd your Air Fryer
9. Cook the pork for about 10 to 12 minutes
10. Serve and enjoy your dish!

AIR FRIED PORK TENDERLOIN WITH PAPRIKA

Prep Time: 10 Minutes | Cooking Time: 20 Minutes | Servings: 4

INGREDIENTS

- 2 pounds of Pork tenderloin
- 2 tbsp of splenda
- 1 tbsp of smoked paprika
- 1 ½ teaspoon of salt
- 1 tsp of ground mustard
- ½ tsp of onion powder
- ½ tsp of ground black pepper
- ¼ tsp of garlic powder
- ¼ tsp of cayenne powder (optional)
- ½ tbsp of olive oil

DIRECTIONS:

1. Mix all your dry ingredients in a large bowl.
2. Start by trimming the pork tenderloin of any excess of fat and silver skin; then coat with about ½ tablespoon of olive oil.
3. Rub the spice mixture over the entire pork tenderloin.
4. Preheat your air fryer to a temperature of about 400° F for about 5 minutes.
5. After about 5 minutes; then carefully place the pork tenderloin into your air fryer and air fry at a temperature of about 400° F for 20 minutes
6. Carefully remove the pork tenderloin to a cutting board; then let rest for about 5 minutes; then slice your meat
7. Serve and enjoy your dish!

AIR FRIED TERIYAKI PORK RIBS

Prep Time:: 8 minutes, cook time: 18 minutes; Serves

INGREDIENTS:

- 1 ½ Pounds of pork ribs
- ½ Teaspoon of salt
- ¼ Teaspoon of white pepper
- 1 and ½ tablespoons of sugar
- ½ Teaspoon of ginger paste
- 1/8 Teaspoon of five spice powder
- 1 Tablespoon of teriyaki sauce
- 1 Tablespoon of light soy sauce
- 2 Finely chopped garlic cloves
- 1 Teaspoon of sugar
- 2 Tablespoons of honey
- 1 Tablespoon of water
- ½ Tablespoon of tomato sauce

DIRECTIONS:

1. Marinate your pork ribs with the prepared marinade and set it aside for overnight
2. Preheat your air fryer to a temperature of 350° F
3. Arrange the pork ribs in the basket steamer of the Air fryer and close the lid
4. Set the timer to 18 minutes and the temperature to 325° F, in the meantime, put a wok on a medium heat and add to it 2 tbsp of olive oil, add the garlic and stir for 2 minutes
5. When the timer of the air fryer beeps, remove the pork ribs
6. Add the pork ribs to the wok and leave it for 2 minutes
7. Serve and enjoy your delicious dish with sauce and white rice.

AIR FRIED MUSTARD CRUSTED PORK

Prep Time: 10 Minutes| Cooking Time: 30 Minutes | Servings: 4

INGREDIENTS

- ¼ cup Dijon mustard
- 2 tablespoons brown sugar
- 1 teaspoon dried parsley flakes
- ½ teaspoon dried thyme
- ¼ tsp salt
- ¼ teaspoon ground black pepper
- 1 ¼ pound pork tenderloin
- ¾ pound small potatoes, halved
- 1 package (12 ounces) fresh green beans, trimmed
- 1 tablespoon olive oil
- salt and ground black pepper to taste

DIRECTIONS:

1. Preheat an air fryer to 400 degrees F (200 degrees C) according to the manufacturer's instructions.
2. Combine mustard, brown sugar, parsley, thyme, salt and pepper in a large bowl. Place tenderloin in bowl and roll in mustard mixture until evenly coated on all sides.
3. Place potatoes, green beans and olive oil in a separate bowl. Season with salt and pepper to taste and stir until combined; then put aside.
4. Place tenderloin in preheated air fryer basket and cook, undisturbed, until lightly pink in center, about 20 minutes. An instant-read thermometer inserted in the center should read at least 145 degrees F (63 degrees C). Transfer to a cutting board and let rest for 10 minutes.
5. Meanwhile, place the green beans and potatoes in the fryer basket and cook for 10 minutes, shaking halfway through.
6. Slice the filet mignon and serve with potatoes and green beans.

AIR FRIED PORK WITH VEGETABLES

Prep Time: 8 Minutes| Cooking Time: 25 Minutes | Servings: 4-5

INGREDIENTS

- 4 yellow bell pepper, cut into pieces
- 2 teaspoons fresh oregano, chopped
- 1 tablespoon olive oil
- 1 uncooked pork shoulder roast (2 pounds)

DIRECTIONS:

1. In a large salad bowl, toss the zucchini, bell pepper and onion (making sure to separate

the onion layers) with 1 tsp salt, 1 tsp pepper, oregano and olive oil.
2. Season the pork loin on all sides with the remaining salt and pepper.
3. Preheat your air fryer appliance by selecting AIR FRY, setting the temperature to 340°F and setting the time to 3 minutes. Select START/STOP to begin.
4. After 3 minutes, place the vegetables in the air fryer basket. Place pork, fat side down, over vegetables; put the pan back in place.
5. Air fry by setting the temperature to 340 F and the time to 25 minutes
6. Select START/STOP to begin.
7. After 10 minutes, flip the pork over. Put the pork back in place to resume cooking
8. Cooking is complete when the internal temperature reaches 140°F. Remove the basket and allow the pork to cool for 5-10 minutes before serving.
9. Serve and enjoy your dish!

AIR FRIED PORK WITH ZUCCHINI

Prep Time: 10 Minutes| Cooking Time: 27 Minutes | Servings: 4

INGREDIENTS

- 1 uncooked boneless pork tenderloin; 2 pounds, halved crosswise
- 1 cup Italian vinaigrette
- 1 eggplant, peeled, cut into 1 inch pieces
- 2 plum tomatoes, diced
- 1 zucchini, cut into half moons
- 1 red bell pepper, diced
- 3 garlic cloves, peeled, minced
- 2 tablespoons extra virgin olive oil
- 1 cup basil
- 2 tablespoons salt, divided

DIRECTIONS:

1. Place the pork loin in a bowl. Toss the pork with the Italian dressing. Cover and refrigerate 2 to 4 hours.
2. In a large bowl, toss the eggplant, tomatoes, zucchini, red onion and garlic with the oil, basil and 1 tbsp salt.
3. Preheat your Air Fryer appliance for about 5 minutes setting the temperature to 390°F and the time to 3 minutes. Select START/STOP to begin.
4. While the Air Fryer preheats, remove the pork from the marinade and season with the remaining tablespoon of salt.
5. Once your Air Fryer is preheated, place the vegetable mixture in the Air Fryer basket. Place the pork over the vegetables.
6. Set the temperature to 380°F, and the time to 20 minutes. Select START/STOP to begin.
7. After 10 minutes, shake the vegetables and turn the pork. Place back the Air Fryer Basket in your Air fryer and cook for 7 additional minutes
8. Serve and enjoy your dish!

AIR FRIED ITALIAN PORK

Prep Time: 10 Minutes| Cooking Time: 27 Minutes | Servings: 4

INGREDIENTS:

- 1 pound Potatoes
- 5 Friggitello (Italian Light Pepper)
- 1 Sliced Onion
- 10 Pork Sausages
- 1 Leaf Of Rosemary
- 1 Leaf Of Oregano
- 1 Tbsp Of Ground Thyme
- 1 Teaspoon Of Paprika
- 1 Teaspoon Ground Cumin
- 1 Tbsp Olive Oil

- 1 Pinch Of Salt To Taste

DIRECTIONS:

1. To start, peel the apples then slice them into small dice. Remove the seeds and white stems from the friggitello peppers and cut lengthwise.
2. Remove the skin from the sausages and cut into slices 1/2 inch thickness.
3. Take a container to put the potatoes, the friggitello and the sliced onion. Season the preparation with salt, spices, rosemary, oregano and thyme. Add a drizzle of oil and mix with a spoon.
4. Put in the basket of the hot air fryer and fry for 20 minutes at 400°F. To ensure that your ingredients cook at the same time, open and shake the basket of the Air fryer.
5. Add the sliced sausages to the fryer and continue to cook at 400°F for 5 minutes. Make sure the potatoes are golden.
6. Remove from the Air fryer and serve with the potatoes with sausages
7. Serve and enjoy your dish!

AIR FRIED PORK

Prep Time: 10 Minutes| Cooking Time: 30 Minutes | Servings: 4-6

INGREDIENTS

- 2 pounds pork filet
- 1 Cup melted butter
- 1 tablespoon olive oil
- A bunch of thyme
- 5 garlic cloves
- 2 tbsp of parsley
- 1 pinch of salt
- 1 pinch of ground black pepper

DIRECTIONS:

1. Mix together the parsley, thyme and garlic. Add the melted butter then salt and pepper. Using a kitchen brush, brush the meat with this mixture, making sure to cover it well
2. For cooking, place the aluminium foil in the bottom of your air fryer to catch all the juices from the meat. Place the pork in your Air Fryer basket and pour the tablespoon of oil just above
3. Cook at a temperature of t 360°F for 30 minutes in order to have medium-rare meat
4. If the cooking does not suit you, add about fifteen minutes.
5. Serve and enjoy your dish!

AIR FRIED PORK CHOPS WITH SWEET POTATOES

Prep Time: 15 Minutes| Cooking Time: 40 Minutes | Servings: 4

INGREDIENTS:

- 2 pound of pork chops
- 1 pinch of salt
- 1 pinch of ground black pepper
- 1 tsp of garlic powder
- 1 tbsp of ground rosemary
- 2 Potatoes
- 2 Sweet potatoes
- 1 tbsp of oil

DIRECTIONS:

1. Take the meat and season with salt and pepper it
2. Preheat your Air Fryer for about 5 minutes to a temperature of 390°F
3. Air fry the pork chops for 20 minutes for 10 minutes per side

4. During this time peel; cut your potatoes, on one side make some to put with your potatoes; the fries with the sweet potatoes.
5. Sprinkle the potatoes with powdered garlic and herbs and remove the meat from your Air Fryer, drizzle the potatoes with a little oil and Air fry for about 15 minutes 360°F
6. Serve and enjoy your dish!

AIR FRIED PORK WITH SAKE

Prep Time: 11 Minutes| Cooking Time: 35 Minutes | Servings: 4

INGREDIENTS:

- 3 Finely chopped garlic cloves
- 1 Tablespoon of sugar
- 2 and ½ tablespoons of Soy Sauce
- 2 Tablespoons of Sake
- 2 Tablespoons of water
- 2 Pork chops
- 1 Pinch of salt
- 1 Pinch of white pepper
- 2 Tablespoons of vegetable oil

DIRECTIONS:

1. Preheat your air fryer to 360° F
2. Thinly slice the garlic and it set aside.
3. Mix the sugar, the Soy Sauce, the Sake and the water into a medium bowl to make a sauce; then set the mixture aside.
4. Sprinkle the salt and the pepper on the beef steaks.
5. Line the pork chops in the basket of the air fryer and drizzle 2 tbsp of oil right on top
6. Add the sliced garlic and close the lid of the air fryer
7. Set the timer to 35 minutes and the temperature to 375 ° F
8. When the timer beeps, unplug the air fryer and remove the beef steaks
9. Place the beef steaks on a serving dish and pour the sauce on the top; then serve and enjoy with garlic and salad of your choice.

AIR FRIED PORK SHOULDER

Prep Time: 15 Minutes| Cooking Time: 30 Minutes | Servings: 4

INGREDIENTS

- 3 Pounds of pork shoulder
- 1 Cup of soy sauce
- 2 Tablespoons of hoisin
- ½ Teaspoon of five spice
- 1 Teaspoon of sriracha or ½ teaspoon of hot pepper
- 1 Cup of brown sugar
- 1 Teaspoon of red food coloring

DIRECTIONS:

1. Cut the pork into cubes of 3 inches each
2. Combine the rest of your ingredients into a bowl until the sugar is completely dissolved
3. Add in the pork.
4. Cover; then marinate your ingredients for overnight and stir from time to time
5. Preheat your air fryer to about 320° F
6. Arrange the pork cubes in the basket of your air fryer and close the lid
7. Set the timer to about 325° F and the heat to 30 minutes
8. When the timer beeps, unplug your air fryer and remove the pork chunks
9. Arrange the pork chunks in a serving dish; then serve and enjoy your meal!

Chapter 11: Fish and Seafood Recipes

AIR FRIED HALIBUT WITH NUTS

Prep Time: 10 Minutes| Cooking Time: 15 Minutes | Servings: 4

INGREDIENTS:

- 2 Fillets of halibut of 6 to 7 oz each
- 3 tbsp of pine nuts
- 2 Tablespoons of Parmesan Cheese
- ¼ Teaspoon of crushed garlic
- 1 Teaspoon of basil pesto
- 1 and ½ tablespoons of mayonnaise

DIRECTIONS

1. Preheat your air fryer to about 390° F
2. Grease a baking pan that fits your air fryer with cooking spray
3. Finely cut the pine nuts and then mince the garlic cloves.
4. Mix altogether the chopped pine nuts with the Parmesan cheese, the minced garlic, the basil pesto, and the mayonnaise
5. With a rubber scraper; spread the mixture of the crust over the surface of the fish
6. Keep piling the mixture of crust until you finish it all
7. Put the fish in the basket of the greased baking tray and put the tray in the basket of the air fryer
8. Close the lid and set the timer to 15 minutes and the temperature to about 390° F
9. When the timer beeps, remove the fish from the air fryer; then serve and enjoy it with lemon wedges

AIR FRIED SHRIMP WITH OREGANO

Prep Time: 10 Minutes| Cooking Time: 10 Minutes | Servings: 4

INGREDIENTS:

- 1 Pound of large and deveined peeled shrimp
- 1 Teaspoon of salt
- 1 Teaspoon of dried and crushed red pepper flakes
- 3 Tablespoons of olive oil
- 1 Medium sliced onion
- 1 Can of cubed tomatoes
- 1 Cup of dry white wine
- 3 Finely chopped garlic cloves
- ¼ Teaspoon of dried oregano leaves
- 3 Tablespoon of chopped Italian parsley leaves
- 3 Tablespoon of chopped basil leaves

DIRECTIONS:

1. Preheat the air fryer to about 365° F
2. In a medium bowl; season the shrimps with 1 pinch of salt and a little bit of red pepper flakes.
3. Grease a baking tray with olive oil and toss the shrimp into your greased baking tray and put it in the basket of the air fryer
4. Close the lid of the air fryer and set the timer to about 3 minutes and the temperature to about 350°F; meanwhile, put the onion in a saucepan and add 2 tablespoons of oil; then sauté for about 2 minutes.
5. Add the wine, the garlic, the oregano and the tomatoes; then let simmer for about 7 minutes
6. Add the shrimps to the tomatoes and add the parsley Add the basil and season with salt

AIR FRIED SALMON WITH SOY SAUCE

Prep Time: 8 Minutes | Cooking Time: 10 Minutes | Servings: 4

INGRDIENTS:

- ½ Cup of vegetable oil
- 1 and ½ tablespoons of rice vinegar
- 1 Teaspoon of sesame oil
- 1/3 Cup of soy sauce
- ¼ Cup of chopped green onions
- 1 Tablespoon of grated fresh ginger root
- 1 Teaspoon of minced garlic
- 4 Skin removed, salmon fillets

DIRECTIONS:

1. In a large plate or bowl, mix altogether the rice vinegar with the sesame oil, the vegetable oil, the soy sauce, the ginger, and the garlic.
2. Put the salmon fillets into your prepared marinade and cover it with a lid or a clean cloth; then set it aside for about 18 minutes
3. Preheat your air fryer to a temperature of about 350° F and put the salmon in the basket of the air fryer; then close the lid and set the timer to about 10 minutes
4. When the timer beeps, remove the salmon from the air fryer; then serve and enjoy it with lemon wedges and rice!

AIR FRIED FISH NUGGETS

Prep Time: 10 Minutes | Cooking Time: 15 Minutes | Servings: 4

INGREDIENTS

- 2 Pounds of fish fillet
- 2 Tbsp of lemon juice
- 3 Tbsp of milk
- 1 Large egg
- 2 Tbsp of Dijon mustard
- 2 Tbsp of yogurt
- 1 Pinch of salt
- 1 Pinch of pepper
- ½ Cup of bread crumbs

DIRECTIONS

1. Preheat your air fryer to about 390° F
2. Line a baking tray with parchment papers
3. Cut the fish fillets into cubes and drizzle with 2 tablespoons of lemon juice.
4. Sprinkle with a little bit of salt and a little bit of pepper.
5. Into a large bowl, combine the milk, the egg, the mustard and the yogurt.
6. Mix your ingredients very well and add season with a little bit of salt
7. Dip your fish nuggets into the mixture of milk and then into the sauce
8. Remove the nuggets from the sauce and with a fork, drain the nuggets of any exceed of the sauce
9. Coat the nuggets with the breadcrumbs and grease a baking tray with cooking spray
10. Put the nuggets in the baking tray and put in the basket of the air fryer; then close the lid
11. Set the timer to about 10 minutes and the temperature to about 375° F
12. When the timer beeps, remove the fish nuggets from the air fryer; then serve and enjoy with tomato sauce

AIR FRIED FISH FILLETS

Prep Time: 10 Minutes | Cooking Time: 8 Minutes | Servings: 4

INGREDIENTS

- 4 white fish fillets
- 1 tablespoon olive oil
- 1 pinch of salt and pepper
- 1 bunch of fresh basil

- 2 cloves garlic
- 2 tablespoons pine nuts
- 1 tablespoon grated parmesan
- 3 tbsp extra virgin olive oil

DIRECTIONS:

1. Preheat your Air fryer to 360°F.
2. Brush the fish fillets with oil, then season with salt and pepper. Place them in the simmering basket of the Air fryer; then slide the simmering basket into the unit. Set the timer for 8 minutes.
3. Pick the basil leaves and place them with the garlic, pine nuts, parmesan and olive oil in a food processor or in a mortar. Mix or grind until you get a sauce. Season with salt to your taste
4. Arrange the fish fillets on a platter and serve them drizzled with the pesto sauce.

Note:

Tip: For variety, you can coat the fish in pesto sauce and breadcrumbs before cooking in the Air Fryer.

AIR FRIED TILAPIA

Prep Time: 10 Minutes| Cooking Time: 7 Minutes | Servings: 4

INGREDIENTS

- 1 ½ pounds tilapia fillet
- ½ tablespoon olive oil (extra virgin)
- 1 tablespoon Cajun seasoning (use my own or store bought)
- 1 lemon (Optional)

DIRECTIONS:

1. Rinse and pat dry the tilapia
2. Preheat your air fryer to 400°F (205°C). Lightly coat the bottom of the basket with cooking oil or use an air fryer liner.
3. Rub a small amount of olive oil on both sides of the fish and sprinkle Cajun seasoning on both sides of the tilapia.
4. ½ tablespoon of olive oil,1 tablespoon Cajun seasoning
5. Place in your preheated air fryer and cook at 400°F (205°C) for 4 minutes, then flip and continue cooking for another 3 minutes.
6. When the fish is cooked, it will be flaky and completely white. Squeeze a little lemon over the fish if you wish and serve immediately, enjoy!
7. 1 lemon

AIR FRIED SALMON WITH PANKO BREADCRUMBS

Prep Time: 10 Minutes| Cooking Time: 10 Minutes | Servings: 4

INGREDIENTS

- 4 salmon fillets, (about 4 ounces each)
- 2 tbsp apple wood Smoked Seasoning
- 2 tbsp Dijon Mustard
- 1/4 cup Panko breadcrumbs

DIRECTIONS:

1. Rub apple wood spice on all sides of salmon. Brush mustard evenly over top of each fillet. Sprinkle the Panko crumbs evenly over the tops of the fillets, pressing gently to ensure adhesion.
2. Place salmon fillets in air fryer basket; avoid stacking fillets. Set temperature to 400°F (200°C).
3. Air fry 7 to 9 minutes or until salmon is cooked through and Panko crumbs are crispy and golden.

AIR FRIED COCONUT AND CHEDDAR CHEESE SHRIMP

Prep Time: 10 Minutes | Cooking Time: 15 Minutes | Servings: 4

INGREDIENTS:

- 1 ½ pounds of whole cooked shrimp
- ½ cup of grated coconut
- 1 lime
- 1 pinch of ground black pepper
- 2 tbsp of olive oil
- 1 pinch of salt
- 1 cup of grated cheddar cheese
- 1 tbsp of fresh and finely minced flat parsley

DIRECTIONS:

1. Shell the shrimps
2. In a salad bowl, mix the prawns with a drizzle of olive oil, the parsley, the lemon juice and the chilli. Salt and pepper Cover and leave to marinate for at least 1 hour (I leave overnight, stirring occasionally).
3. Generously roll your shrimp without draining them in the coconut; then into the cheddar cheese
4. Preheat the Air fryer to 400°F.
5. Place the shrimp in the basket and cook for 15 minutes, shaking occasionally.
6. Serve and enjoy your delicious dish!

AIR FRIED FROZEN SHRIMP

Prep Time: 10 Minutes | Cooking Time: 8 Minutes | Servings: 4

INGREDIENTS

- 2 pounds of frozen shrimp
- 1 tbsp of vegetable oil (spray bottle or drizzle)
- 1 tsp sea salt
- 2-4 lemon wedges (Optional)

DIRECTIONS:

1. Preheat your air fryer to 400°F (205°C). Lightly coat your fryer with cooking oil.
2. Add the frozen shrimp straight from the bag to the basket or air fryer rack.
3. Arrange the shrimp in a single layer.
4. Bake the shrimp at 400°F (205°C) for about 4-5 minutes, then open your air fryer and flip the shrimp.
5. Continue cooking for another 4 to 5 minutes. Check if the prawns are completely cooked, if not, flip them in your air fryer for another 1-2 minutes.
6. Carefully remove from air fryer and let cool slightly. Season to taste with salt, serve with lemon wedges and cocktail sauce if desired
7. Serve and enjoy your dish!

AIR FRIED FISH AND CHIPS

Prep Time: 7 Minutes | Cooking Time: 10 Minutes | Servings: 4

INGREDIENTS:

- 8 fish fillets (Cod, Haddock, Tilapia, Pollock or other white fish)
- Oil spray
- 2 beaten eggs
- 1/2 cup flour
- 2 cups (500 mL) panko breadcrumbs
- 1/2 teaspoon onion powder
- 1/2 teaspoon garlic powder
- 1/2 teaspoon Old Bay spice
- 1/2 tsp Salt
- 1/4 teaspoon pepper

DIRECTIONS:

1. In a bowl, combine the breadcrumbs and spices. Put aside.
2. In another bowl, beat the eggs.
3. Then, in a third bowl, add the flour.
4. Drain the fish fillets well with paper towel.

5. Dip each fillet in the flour, then in the eggs.
6. Drain excess; then dip in breadcrumbs.
7. Spray fillets and air fryer basket well with oil.
8. Preheat air fryer to 390°F (200°C).
9. Cook for 8 to 10 minutes. Flip and spray a little more oil halfway through cooking.
10. Serve with tartar sauce
11. Enjoy your dish!

AIR FRIED CURRIED PRAWNS

Prep Time: 10 Minutes| Cooking Time: 8 Minutes | Servings: 4

INGREDIENTS:

- 2 pounds prawns
- 3 cloves of garlic
- 1 tsp ginger
- 1 tsp curry
- 1/2 tsp hot pepper
- 1 tsp of fresh coriander
- 2 tbsp of olive oil

DIRECTIONS:

1. Prepare a marinade by mixing the shelled prawns, curry, ginger, chopped coriander, olive oil. Leave to marinate for 1 hour in the fridge.
2. Heat your Air fryer for 5 minutes to 400°F
3. Place the prawns in your Air fryer basket and cook for 7 to 8 minutes
4. Remove the prawns from your Air fryer

AIR FRIED SCALLOPS

Prep Time: 5 Minutes| Cooking Time: 10 Minutes | Servings: 4

INGREDIENTS

- 12 fresh scallops
- ½ tsp of sea salt
- ¼ tsp of ground black pepper
- 3 Tbsp of butter
- 1 garlic clove, minced
- 1 tbsp of lemon juice
- 1 tsp of chopped fresh chives

DIRECTIONS:

1. Rinse and thoroughly pat dry your scallops.
2. On both sides, season the scallops with salt and pepper.
3. Spray your air fryer basket with cooking spray and properly distribute the scallops in it without crowding it; you can cook in batches.
4. Air Fry your scallops for 10 minutes at 400°F, flipping halfway through.
5. While the scallops are frying, melt the butter in the microwave or on the stovetop with the garlic. Combine the lemon juice and chives in a mixing bowl.
6. When the scallops are done, lay them on a platter and sprinkle with the lemon garlic butter. Serve right away.

AIR FRIED FISH TACOS

Prep Time: 5 Minutes| Cooking Time: 10 Minutes | Servings: 4

INGREDIENTS

- 2 pounds (2 lbs) fresh cod or haddock or frozen fish, thawed and patted dry
- 1 cup of seasoned flour mix
- ½ cup flour or gluten-free cornmeal
- 1 tsp smoked paprika
- ½ tsp oregano
- ¼ tsp Ancho chili or cayenne pepper (to taste)

For the egg mix:

- 2 beaten eggs
- 2 tbsp white beer or Ale or milk
- 1 ½ cups of Breadcrumbs

- 2 cups crumbled potato chips
- 1 pinch of salt and Vinegar or Jalapeno

To serve with:

- 4 blue corn tortillas
- 1 tsp of fresh coriander
- Shredded red cabbage
- 1 diced mango

For the Salsa verde:

- 1 Avocado, and roasted tomato salsa or guacamole
- pico de gallo

DIRECTIONS:

1. Cut the fish fillets into pieces and pat them dry on absorbent paper. Add the beer and yeast. Mix well with a whisk and leave to stand for an hour.
2. Prepare the three stages for the breading.
3. Combine the flour, paprika, oregano and chilli in a bowl.
4. Beat the egg with the beer or milk in a second bowl.
5. Crush the chips in a third bowl.
6. Dip successively in the three bowls
7. Place the fish pieces in the air fryer basket. Cook 6 to 7 minutes depending on the size of the fish
8. On each tortilla warmed in the plate, spread the salsa of your choice, place the pieces of breaded fish, garnish with cilantro, cabbage, mango and pico de gallo according to your mood!

AIR FRIED CORN ON THE COB WITH LOBSTERS

Prep Time: 5 Minutes| Cooking Time: 10 Minutes | Servings: 4

INGREDIENTS

- 10 fresh Corn on the cob, cut into halves
- 1 ½ Pounds of fresh shrimp (or frozen)
- 1 pound of cut-in-half lobster tails (fresh or frozen)
- 2 tbsp of melted butter
- 1 pinch of salt
- 1 pinch of ground black Pepper, black
- 1 tbsp of Cajun seasoning or Old Bay seasoning

DIRECTIONS:

1. Start by putting the seafood boil, the butter, and the spices in your Air Fryer Basket.
2. Preheat your Air Fryer to 400°F and use your air fryer by setting the timer to 10 minutes
3. Once the timer beeps, remove your ingredients from the Air Fryer

AIR FRIED SQUID RINGS

Prep Time: 5 Minutes| Cooking Time: 10 Minutes | Servings: 4

INGREDIENTS

- 2 pounds of fresh squid rings
- ½ pound of flour
- 1 tablespoon olive oil
- 2 onions
- 1 pinch of salt

DIRECTIONS:

1. Roll the fresh calamari in flour and salt, and then set aside.
2. Cut the onions into small dice and distribute in the Air fryer basket with the drizzle of olive oil.
3. Start your Air Fryer program at 360°F for 5 minutes and let heat for 5 minutes
4. When the Air Fryer makes a sound or beep, you can add the squid rings.
5. Close the lid and cook in your Air Fryer for about 25 minutes

Chapter 12: Vegan Recipes

AIR FRIED TOMATO WITH HERBS

Prep Time: 6 Minutes | Cooking Time: 20 Minutes | Servings: 4

INGREDIENTS

- 1 ½ Pounds of tomatoes
- 1 Pinch of salt
- 1 Pinch of pepper
- 2 Tablespoons of olive oil
- 1 tsp of herbs, rosemary

DIRECTIONS:

1. Preheat your air fryer to about 325° F
2. Wash the tomatoes and cut it into halves
3. Turn the tomato on the other side and grease the bottom with a drizzle of cooking spray
4. Turn all the halves of the tomatoes and season it with a pinch of black pepper, parsley, basil, oregano, thyme, rosemary and sage
5. Put the tomato halves in a greased baking tray hat fits your air fryer; then put it in the basket of the air fryer and close the lid and set the timer to about 20 minutes and the temperature to about 325° F
6. When the timer beeps, remove the tomatoes from the air fryer; and serve

AIR FRIED CAULIFLOWER BAKE

Prep Time: 10 Minutes | Cooking Time: 25 Minutes | Servings: 4

INGREDIENTS:

- ½ Pound of cooked cauliflower florets
- ¼ Cup of raw soaked cashews
- 2 Tablespoons of nutritional yeast
- 1 and ½ tablespoons of cornstarch
- ¼ Teaspoon of garlic powder
- ½ Teaspoon of onion powder
- ¼ Teaspoon of salt
- 1 Pinch of freshly ground black pepper
- 1 Cup of unsweetened almond milk

DIRECTIONS

1. Preheat your air fryer to about 350° F
2. Grease a baking pan that fits your air fryer with cooking spray
3. Spread your cooked broccoli in the bottom of the tray; then start preparing your sauce
4. Mix the cashews with the nutritional yeast, the cornstarch, the garlic powder, the onion, the salt, the black pepper and the water into a food processor
5. Blend your ingredients until it becomes smooth
6. Pour the sauce of the cashew over your vegetables; then arrange your cauliflower florets on top of it
7. Put the baking pan in the air fryer basket; then close the lid
8. Set the timer to about 20 minutes and the temperature to around 375° F
9. When the timer beeps, remove the baking pan from the air fryer and set it aside to cool for 7 minutes
10. Serve and enjoy!

AIR FRIED ZUCCHINI PATTIES WITH CASHEW CHEESE

Prep Time: 10 Minutes | Cooking Time: 15 Minutes | Servings: 4

INGREDIENTS

- 1 and ½ pounds of zucchini
- ½ Teaspoon of salt
- 2 Large beaten pasteurized vegan eggs
- 6 Tablespoons of cashew cheese
- 1 Minced or pressed garlic clove
- ¼ Cup of vegan butter

DIRECTIONS:

1. Start by combining the coarsely shred zucchini with 1 pinch of salt and 1 pinch of black ground pepper into a large bowl
2. Set the ingredients aside for about 15 minutes; then squeeze it with both your hands in order to press any excess of moisture
3. Add in the eggs, the cashew cheese and the garlic
4. Grease a baking paper that fits your air fryer basket with butter
5. Spoon 1 and ½ tablespoons of the zucchini mixture in your greased baking paper and slightly flatten it; then repeat the same process with the remaining mixture until you finish it all
6. Put the baking paper in the basket of the air fryer and close the lid
7. Set the timer to about 10 minutes and the temperature to about 375° F
8. When the timer beeps, remove the baking paper from the air fryer and set it aside for about 10 minutes to cool; then serve and enjoy it.

AIR FRIED KALE NUGGETS

Prep Time: 10 Minutes | Cooking Time: 15 Minutes | Servings: 4

INGREDIENTS

- 2 Cups of finely chopped potatoes
- 1 Teaspoon of extra-virgin olive oil
- 1 Minced garlic clove
- 4 Cups of coarsely chopped kale
- ⅛ Cup of almond milk
- ¼ Teaspoon of sea salt
- ⅛ Teaspoon of ground black pepper
- 1 tbsp of vegetable oil

DIRECTIONS:

1. Place the potatoes in a pan filled with water
2. Cook your potatoes for about 25 minutes until it becomes tender
3. Heat the oil in a skillet over a medium high heat; then add the garlic and sauté for about 2 minutes
4. Add in the kale and sauté it for 2 minutes; then transfer the mixture to a bowl
5. Drain the potatoes and transfer it to a bowl and add in the milk, the salt and the pepper
6. Mash the mixture with a potato masher
7. Transfer the potatoes a large bowl and combine it with the cooked kale.
8. Preheat your air fryer to a temperature of about 390°F for about 5 minutes.
9. Roll the mixture of the kale and the potatoes into nuggets of about 1 inch each
10. Spray your Air Fryer basket with cooking spray
11. Carefully arrange the nuggets in your Air Fryer basket
12. Lock your Air fryer and cook for about 15 minutes and shake each 5 minutes
13. When the timer beeps; turn off your Air Fryer

AIR FRIED EGGPLANT FRITTERS

Prep Time: 10 Minutes | Cooking Time: 15 Minutes | Servings: 4

INGREDIENTS:

- 2 Medium sized Eggplants
- ¼ cup of Cornstarch
- ¼ cup of Olive Oil
- ¼ cup of Water
- 1 pinch of Salt

DIRECTIONS:

1. Preheat your Air fryer to a degree of 390°F.
2. Cut the eggplants to slices of 10 mm in each.
3. In a big bowl, mix all together the cornstarch,
4. Add the olive oil, the water, and the eggplants
5. Slowly, coat the eggplants
6. Put half the quantity of the eggplant fries in the air fryer
7. Cook the components for around 12 to 13 minutes or until you see eggplant slices start to get brown.
8. Repeat this process until you see all the eggplant fries are perfectly cooked.
9. Serve and enjoy your meal!

AIR FRIED VEGGIES WITH OLIVE AND CORIANDER

Prep Time: 15 Minutes | Cooking Time: 8 Minutes | Servings: 4

INGREDIENTS:

- 1 ½ Pounds OF tomatoes
- 1 pound of green pepper
- 1 medium onion
- 3 cloves of garlic
- ½ tbsp of salt
- 1 tbsp of Coriander powder
- 1 tbsp of lemon juice
- 1tbsp of olive oil
- 1 cup of black olive

DIRECTIONS:

1. Preheat your Air fryer to 350°F
2. Line the pepper, the tomato and the onion in the basket
3. Slide the basket in the Air Fryer
4. Lock the lid and set your time to 8 minutes
5. Open up the lid of the air fryer, then flip the vegetables to the other side
6. Lock the lid of the air fryer again
7. After 5 minutes, remove the vegetables from the air fryer
8. Peel the skin of the vegetables
9. Place the vegetables in a blender or a mortar with the salt, the coriander powder and process it
10. Drizzle with olive oil
11. Serve and enjoy your dish!

Chapter 13: Bread Recipes

WHOLE WHEAT ALMOND BREAD

Prep Time: 15 Minutes| Cooking Time: 20 Minutes | Servings: 4

INGREDIENTS

- 1 Pound of wheat flour
- 1 ½ tbsp of dried or fresh yeast
- 2 ½ cups lukewarm water
- 1 tbsp caster sugar
- 1 pinch of salt
- 1 cup of sunflower seeds
- 1 cup Pumpkin seeds
- 1 cup of almonds, slivered

DIRECTIONS:

1. Prepare the dough before letting it rise: mix the seeds, almonds, and the flour, add the salt, the sugar and the yeast.
2. Knead the dough until you get a smooth ball.
3. Let the dough rest covered with a cloth near a heat source.
4. After 30 to 60 min the dough is rested.
5. Preheat your Air fryer to 400°F
6. After airing the dough, place it in the mold of your fryer with baking paper in the bottom.
7. Moisten the top of the dough with a little water.
8. Cook in your Air fryer for 15 to 20 minutes, until it has a golden crust.
9. Serve and enjoy your bread!

WALNUT BREAD

Prep Time: 10 Minutes| Cooking Time: 40 Minutes | Servings: 5

INGREDIENTS:

- 2 ¼ Cups of all purpose flour
- ½ Cup of chopped Walnuts
- 2 Teaspoons of Gluten-free baking powder
- 2 Teaspoons of Cinnamon
- ¼ Teaspoon of sea salt
- 6 Tablespoons of butter
- ½ Cup of Erythritol
- 4 Large beaten Eggs
- ¼ Cup of Milk
- 2 Teaspoons of Banana extract

DIRECTIONS:

1. Preheat your air fryer to about 350° F.
2. Line a loaf baking pan with a parchment paper; in the meantime, combine the flour, the baking powder, the cinnamon, and the sea salt.
3. In a separate bowl, mix the erythritol and the butter; then crack in the eggs and whisk very well
4. Add the banana extract and the milk.
5. Pour your dry ingredients into the wet ingredients and mix on a low speed.
6. Add in the walnuts and put the batter in your lined loaf tray; then press
7. Top with walnuts and put the loaf tray in the basket of the air fryer and close the lid
8. Set the timer to about 40 minutes and the temperature to 365° F
9. When the timer beeps, remove the loaf of bread from the air fryer
10. Serve and enjoy!

CRISPY VANILLA BREAD

Prep Time: 10 Minutes| Cooking Time: 8 Minutes | Servings: 4

INGREDIENTS

- 4 to 5 slices of bread
- 2 large eggs
- 1/3 cup whole milk

- 1 tbsp vanilla extract
- 1 tsp of ground cinnamon
- 3 tbsp sugar

DIRECTIONS:

1. Slice the bread into thirds or quarters depending on the width of the bread to obtain sticks of 1 ½ to 2 inches.
2. In a small bowl, combine the eggs, milk and vanilla. Whisk well to combine and set aside.
3. In another small bowl, combine the cinnamon and sugar; then mix your ingredients very well.
4. Dip each slice of bread in egg mixture and coat both sides. Let the excess mixture drip off and place on a plate or parchment paper; generously sprinkle cinnamon and sugar on both sides of the bread.
5. Spray air fryer basket with oil. Place the sticks and avoid them touching each other.
6. Preheat air fryer to 350°F.
7. Bake 4 minutes, or until top is lightly browned.
8. Flip and cook an additional 2 to 4 minutes, or until desired level of crispiness.
9. Leave to cool for several minutes, then enjoy with syrup, powdered sugar or berries
10. Serve and enjoy your bread!

PUMPKIN AND CINNAMON SWIRL BREAD

Prep Time: 10 Minutes| Cooking Time: 40 Minutes | Servings: 5

INGREIDENTS:

- 2 large, beaten eggs
- ¼ cp of milk
- ¼ cp of pumpkin purée
- ⅛ teaspoon of pumpkin pie spices
- 4 slices of cinnamon swirl bread
- A little bit of butter and pecan syrup to use for serving

DIRECTIONS:

1. In a large bowl, mix all together the large eggs, the milk, the pumpkin and the pie spice and don't stop whisking until you obtain a smooth mixture.
2. Dip both sides of the bread, each separately in the mixture of the eggs.
3. Place the rack inside the Air Fryer's cooking basket.
4. Place two of the slices of the bread on the Air Fryer Basket
5. Set the temperature up to 340° F and set your time for 10 exact minutes.
6. When the Cooking Time: is completed, repeat the same process with the remaining slices you have.
7. When the pumpkin pie is totally, serve it with butter and enjoy your meal.

AIR FRIED SEED BREAD

Prep Time: 10 Minutes| Cooking Time: 40 Minutes | Servings: 5

INGREDIENTS

- 2 ½ cups whole wheat flour
- ½ sachet of baker's yeast (1 tbsp g)
- 1 cup sunflower seeds and/or pumpkin seeds
- A small pizza pan or a shallow cake pan 15cm in diameter

DIRECTIONS:

1. In a bowl, mix the two flours with 1 teaspoon of salt, the yeast and the seeds. Add 1 ½ cups of lukewarm water, continuing to mix until the mixture forms a soft ball.
2. Knead the dough for about 5 minutes until smooth and elastic. Form a ball with the dough and place it in a bowl. Cover with cling film and let rise in a warm place for 30 minutes.

3. Preheat your Air fryer to 400°F. Moisten the top of the dough with a brush.
4. Place the cake tin in the air fryer basket and insert it into the air fryer. Set the timer for 18 minutes and bake the bread until it takes on a nice golden color. Let it cool on a wire rack.

AIR FRIED ROSEMARY BREAD

Prep Time: 20 Minutes | Cooking Time: 25 Minutes | Servings: 5

INGREDIENTS:

- 1 ½ cups of milk
- 1 packet of dry baker's yeast
- 3 cups of flour
- 2 tbsp of olive oil
- 1 tbsp dried rosemary
- 1 tsp salt

DIRECTIONS:

1. Place the milk, ½ cup of water and the baker's yeast in a stainless steel bowl then mix very well
2. Add in the milk and the baker's yeast.
3. Add in the rest of your ingredients and mix very well; then knead your mixture
4. Add in the flour, the olive oil.
5. Take the dough out of the stainless steel bowl and let it rest in a ball, in a hollow dish covered with a damp cloth for 2 hours, at room temperature
6. Preheat your Air Fryer to a temperature of 400°F for 5 minutes
7. Take your dough and divide it into four. Form about 4 balls, place them on a greased baking paper and line it in your Air Fryer basket
8. Place the baking paper in your Air Fryer Basket and arrange the bread on the paper
9. Air fry your bread for about 20 to 25 minutes
10. Remove the bread from the Air Fryer; then serve and enjoy hot!

AIR FRIED BROWN BREAD

Prep Time: 10 Minutes | Cooking Time: 40 Minutes | Servings: 4

INGREDIENT:

- 2 pounds large loaf
- 1½ cups of room temperature water
- 1 tbsp olive oil
- 1½ tsp kosher salt
- 1 1/2 tsp honey
- 1 tbsp rosemary, fresh and chopped
- 2½ cups unbleached all-purpose flour
- 1½ cup whole wheat flour
- 1/3 cup of rye flour
- 1½ tsp active, instant or bread machine dry yeast
- 1 ½ cups Kalamata olives, pitted, drained, patted dry and halved

DIRECTIONS:

1. Put all the ingredients (except the olives), in the order listed, into a large bowl
2. Add in the olives and mix very well
3. Knead your mixture very well
4. At the end of the cycle, remove the pan from the robot, transfer the bread to a wire rack and let it cool completely before slicing.

AIR FRIED GARLIC BREAD

Prep Time: 12 Minutes | Cooking Time: 6 Minutes | Servings: 4

INGREDIENTS

- 2 French loaves of bread
- 8 tbsp Butter (softened, unsalted)
- 3 tablespoon grated parmesan
- 1 teaspoon Italian seasoning
- ½ tsp minced garlic (finely minced)
- ½ teaspoon each, salt and pepper

DIRECTIONS:

1. Preheat your air fryer to 360°F (182°C)
2. Cut your loaf in half and then again lengthwise or into slices small enough to fit in Air the fryer.
3. In a small bowl, add butter, Parmesan, minced garlic, Italian seasoning, salt and pepper. Mix your ingredients very well.
4. Combine 8 tablespoon of butter,3 tablespoons of grated parmesan,1 teaspoon of Italian seasoning,½ teaspoon minced garlic,½ teaspoon each, salt and pepper; spread the mixture on the bread loaf, place the bread in your Air fryer basket and bake at a temperature of 360°F (182°C) for 4-6 minutes or until golden brown and bubbly.
5. Add a minute or two for extra crispy garlic bread.
6. Remove the bread from the air fryer, serve and enjoy your bread!

AIR FRIED QUICK BREAD

Prep Time: 10 Minutes| Cooking Time: 20 Minutes | Servings: 4

INGREDIENTS

- 2 cups of bread flour
- 1 cup of spelled flour
- 1 cup of sourdough starter
- 1 tablespoon of extra virgin olive oil
- ½ teaspoon of fine sea salt
- 1 cup of water

DIRECTIONS:

1. Combine all together the bread flour, the spelled flour, the sourdough, the oil and the salt in the bowl of a stand mixer. Start kneading your dough using the dough hook. Add in the water until all your ingredients combine very well and start to come together; you may not need all the water. Knead at low speed for about 5 minutes.
2. Fold in the dough into a ball. Place the dough in your air fryer ovenproof dish. Cover your dough with a plastic wrap and let double in size, for about 5 hours to an overnight.
3. Preheat your air fryer to a temperature of 390 degrees F (200 degrees C). Remove the plastic film and mark the bread.
4. Place your baking dish in your air fryer and bake until the bread is golden brown, about 20 minutes. An instant-read thermometer inserted in the center should read at least 190 degrees F (88 degrees C). Let your bread cool before slicing.
5. Serve and enjoy your bread!

AIR FRIED ORANGE ALMOND BREAD

Prep Time: 10 Minutes| Cooking Time: 25 Minutes | Servings: 4-5

INGREDIENTS:

- 4 Large eggs
- 2/3 Cup of ghee, melted
- 1 tsp of pink salt
- 1 Cup of all purpose flour
- 4 oranges, juices
- 1 tsp of baking powder
- ½ cup of sesame
- 1 cup of almonds, roasted and chopped

DIRECTIONS:

1. Whisk the eggs, the melted ghee and the salt in a large bowl
2. Add in the orange juice, and the almonds, then whisk in the flour and the baking powder
3. Once the mixture is smooth, grease the baking pan of your Air Fryer with cooking spray or a loaf pan that fits your Air Fryer basket

4. Pour the mixture in a greased mini loaf tin
5. Top your bread with the sesame
6. Cover your Air Fryer pan with an aluminium foil
7. Place the Air Fryer pan in your Air Fryer basket and close the lid
8. Set your timer to about 25minutes and set the temperature to about 370° F
9. Remove the bread pan from the Air Fryer and let cool for 6 minutes
10. Slice your bread; then serve and enjoy it!

AIR FRIED BUTTER BREAD

Prep Time: 15Minutes| Cooking Time: 20 Minutes | Servings: 4

INGREDIENTS

- 2 tablespoons of unsalted butter melted, plus more for the pan
- 1 1/2 teaspoons of active dry yeast
- 1 1/2 teaspoons of sugar
- 1 1/2 teaspoons of kosher salt
- 2 2/3 cups of all-purpose flour

DIRECTIONS:

1. Grease a circular baking tray that fits your Air Fryer basket and set it aside
2. In a stand mixer fitted with the dough hook attachment, combine the butter, yeast, sugar, salt, and 1 cup of warm water. Add in about 1/2 cup of the all purpose flour at a time to your mixer on low speed, allowing for each addition to be thoroughly integrated before adding more flour. After adding all the quantity of the flour, knead for 8 minutes on medium speed.
3. Transfer your dough to the prepared pan, cover, and let aside for 1 hour to double in size.
4. Set your air fryer to 380 degrees F and place the pan with the dough inside. Cook for about 20 minutes, or until the bread is dark brown and the interior temperature reaches 200 degrees F.
5. Allow to cool in the pan for 5 minutes before turning out onto a rack to cool fully.
6. Serve and enjoy your bread

AIR FRIED FOCCACIA BREAD WITH OLIVES

Prep Time: 15 Minutes| Cooking Time: 15 Minutes | Servings: 6

INGREDIENTS

- 4 Eggs
- 2 heaped tbsp of plain whole milk
- 1/3 Cup and 1 tbsp of all purpose flour
- 2 and 1/2 tbsp of whole Psyllium husks
- 1/2 tsp of salt
- 1 tsp of gluten-free baking powder
- Toppings:
- 1/4 Cup of sliced Kalamata olives
- 2 tbsp of minced herbs
- 2 tbsp of extra virgin olive oil
- 1 Pinch of salt

DIRECTIONS:

1. Preheat your Air Fryer to a temperature of about 375° F
2. Line your baking pan with a parchment paper.
3. Mix the eggs with the yogurt
4. Add the dry ingredients to the wet ingredients and combine with your hands until you obtain a thick round ball of dough
5. Transfer the prepared dough to your baking sheet and spread the dough into a rectangle of about 1/2 inch of thickness
6. Add in the herbs, the olives, the olive oil; 1 pinch of salt in a skillet and heat it over a medium high
7. Top your dough with the mixture of the olives and drizzle with the olive oil

8. Place the baking pan in your Air Fryer and lock the lid
9. Set the timer for about 15 minutes and set the temperature to 375° F
10. When the timer beeps; turn off your Air Fryer and remove the pan aside to cool
11. Slice your bread, then serve and enjoy it!

AIR FRIED GARLIC BAGELS

Prep Time: 10Minutes| Cooking Time: 23 Minutes | Servings: 4

INGREDIENTS

- 5 Oz of cream cheese to the room temperature
- 4 tbsp of butter
- 1 Egg
- ¼ Minced white onion
- ½ tbsp of minced garlic
- ¼ tsp of salt
- ½ tbsp of Baking powder
- 2 tbsp of bagel seasoning

DIRECTIONS

1. Preheat your Air Fryer to a temperature of about oven 350° F
2. Grease a silicone donut mould that fits your Air Fryer basket
3. Combine the cream cheese with the butter and the eggs in a large mixer
4. Add the salt, the garlic, the onion, and the baking powder to your mixture and mix very well
5. Distribute your batter into a silicone donut mold of 6 holes
6. Place the donut mold in your Air Fryer basket and lock the lid
7. Set the timer to about 16 to 17 minutes and set the temperature to 375° F
8. When the timer beeps; turn off your Air Fryer; then remove the mold and set it aside to cool for 5 minutes

AIR FRIED SESAME BUNS

Prep Time: 10Minutes| Cooking Time: 30 Minutes | Servings: 4

INGREDIENTS

- 1 Cup of all purpose flour
- 1 Cup of sesame seeds
- ½ Cup of pumpkin seeds
- ½ Cup of Psyllium powder
- 1 Cup of hot water
- 1 tbsp of Celtic sea salt
- 1 tbsp of baking powder
- Large egg whites

DIRECTIONS

1. Pre-heat your Air Fryer to a temperature of about 350° F
2. Start by combining all your dry ingredients in a bowl
3. Mix your ingredients very well.
4. Now, whisk the egg whites until it becomes foamy
5. Add the egg white to your dry ingredients and combine very well with a large spoon
6. The dough you obtain should be crumbly
7. Pour in the water; then stir until you start noticing the dough to be smooth
8. Sprinkle the sesame over a platter
9. Form buns from the dough; then arrange the buns into the sesame-sprinkled platter and press it very well so that the sesame would stick
10. Line your Air Fryer pan with a baking sheet and spray it with cooking spray
11. Arrange the balls in the Air Fryer pan lined with the parchment paper
12. Place the pan in your Air Fryer and lock the lid
13. Set the timer for about 30 minutes and set the temperature to 360° F

14. When the timer beeps, turn off your Air Fryer and check the donuts for doneness
15. Serve and enjoy your buns!

AIR FRIED SPICY BAGELS

Prep Time: 12 Minutes| Cooking Time: 25 Minutes | Servings: 6

INGREDIENTS

- 2 Cups of grated Mozzarella cheese
- 2 Oz of Cream cheese
- 1 ½ cups of all purpose flour
- 1 teaspoon baking powder
- 3 Jalapeno peppers
- 2 Large Eggs

DIRECTIONS:

1. Preheat your Air Fryer to a temperature of about 200° C/400° F
2. Deseed the jalapeno peppers and dice the jalapeno
3. Slice the peppers into circles; then set it aside
4. Combine the flour with the baking powder in a large bowl
5. Add in the eggs and the diced jalapeno peppers and mix very well
6. In a separate bowl; mix the cream cheese with the mozzarella
7. Microwave the mozzarella for about 2 minutes; then add it to the mixture of the flour and combine the mixture very well
8. Break the batter into about 6 pieces; then roll the dough pieces into the shape of bagels
9. Decorate your bagels with the sliced jalapenos and sprinkle with some grated Cheddar cheese.
10. Spray your Air Fryer Pan with cooking spray
11. Arrange the bagels in the Air Fryer pan and place it in your Air Fryer
12. Lock the lid and set the timer to about 25 minutes and the temperature to about 375° F
13. When the timer beeps; turn off your Air Fryer and set the bagels aside for about 5 minutes
14. Eat and enjoy your bagels!

CHEESE BREAD

Prep Time: 15 Minutes| Cooking Time: 20 Minutes | Servings: 4-6

INGREDIENTS

- 5 Oz of softened cream cheese
- ¼ Cup of softened butter
- 2cups of all purpose flour
- 2 tsp of baking powder
- ½ tsp of sea salt
- ½ Cup of shredded Parmesan cheese shredded
- 3 tbsp of water
- 3 large eggs
- ½ Cup of shredded mozzarella cheese shredded

DIRECTIONS:

1. Preheat your Air Fryer to a temperature of about 400°F.
2. Spray a loaf pan of about 8x4-inch with cooking spray
3. Combine the cream cheese and the butter with a mixer or a food processor.
4. Add the remaining ingredients and process it very well
5. Spread the batter in your greased bread tin
6. Place the loaf pan in your Air Fryer basket and lock the lid
7. Set the timer to 20 minutes and set the temperature to 200° C/400° F
8. When the timer beeps; turn off your Air Fryer
9. Remove the loaf pan from your Air Fryer and set it aside to cool for 10 minutes
10. Slice the bread; then serve and enjoy it

Chapter 14: Dessert Recipes

AIR FRIED FLAN

Prep Time: 12 Minutes | Cooking Time: 15 Minutes | Servings:: 4

INGREDIENTS:

- ½ Cup of agave syrup
- 1 and ½ tablespoons of Water
- ¾ Cup of canned Milk
- ¼ Cup of Evaporated Milk
- ¼ Cup of unsweetened Condensed Milk
- 2 Beaten whole Eggs
- 1 Yolk of egg.

DIRECTIONS:

1. Coat about 5 ramekins or a round baking tray with vegetable oil
2. Preheat your Air Fryer to about 325°F.
3. Pour 2 cups of boiling water into your preheated Air fryer.
4. In a saucepan, put the sugar with 1 and ½ tablespoons of water and cook over a low heat; but make sure to swirl the pan and let cook for 9 minutes
5. Pour about 2 tablespoons of caramel in the bottom of serving cups.
6. In a separate large mixing bowl, combine the milk with the egg yolk and the eggs
7. Once your ingredients are very-well blended, put the custard into the base of your ramekins and pour in the batter into the ramekins
8. Cover your ramekins with an aluminium foil tin; then bake it the Air Fryer for about 30 minutes and set the temperature to about 350° F
9. When the timer beeps, remove the ramekins from the air fryer and let it rest for about 10 minutes
10. Top the flan with coconut flakes and mango orange sauce

AIR FRIED CHOCOLATE BARS

Prep Time: 12 Minutes | Cooking Time: 15 Minutes | Servings: 4

INGREDIENTS:

- 2 and ¾ cups of quick oats
- ½ Teaspoon of salt
- ½ Cup of pure maple syrup
- ¼ Cup of peanut butter
- 1 Tablespoon of water
- 1 Teaspoon of pure vanilla extract
- 5 Oz of chocolate chips
- ½ Cup of peanut butter

DIRECTIONS:

1. Start by lining a baking tray with a parchment paper; then set it aside
2. In a bowl, combine the maple syrup with the ¼ cup of peanut butter, the water, and the vanilla until it becomes smooth.
3. Add the salt and the oats; then transfer the 2/3 of your batter and press it down with another sheet of parchment paper into the bottom of the tray
4. Put the tray in the basket of the air fryer and set the timer for about 5 minutes and the temperature to about 320° F
5. When the timer beeps, remove the tray from the air fryer and set it aside to cool
6. In another bowl, melt the peanut butter and the chocolate; then stir very well
7. Pour the melted chocolate above the crust in the tray and top with the crumbled oats
8. Put the tray in the refrigerator for about 10 minutes
9. Cut your dessert into squares; then serve and enjoy its delicious taste!

AIR FRIED CHOCOLATE MUFFINS

Prep Time: 12 Minutes | Cooking Time: 15 Minutes | Servings: 4

INGREDIENTS

- 2 and ½ cups of rolled oats
- 1 and ¼ cups of mashed ripe banana
- ¼ Cup of pure maple syrup
- 2/3 Cup of water
- 2 and ½ tablespoons of oil
- 1 and ½ teaspoon of pure vanilla extract
- ½ Teaspoon of salt
- ¼ Cup of cocoa powder
- ½ Cup of chocolate chips
- 2 Tablespoons of Chia seeds
- ½ Cup of shredded raisins

DIRECTIONS

1. Preheat your air fryer to about 380° F.
2. Line a cupcake pan of about 11 cupcake tins with paper liners
3. In a large and deep bowl, mix altogether the dry ingredients.
4. In another bowl, mix the wet ingredients and stir very well into your dry mixture
5. Pour the batter into your liners and put it into the basket of the air fryer; then close the lid
6. Set the timer to about 15 minutes and the temperature to 365° F
7. When the timer beeps, remove the muffins from the air fryer and set it aside for about 10 minutes
8. Serve and enjoy!

AIR FRIED VANILLA CAKE

Prep Time: 10 Minutes | Cooking Time: 35 Minutes | Servings: 4

INGREDIENTS:

- ½ Cup of softened butter
- 1 Cup of granulated erythritol sweetener
- 3 Large eggs
- 1 Teaspoon of vanilla extract
- 1 and ½ cups of superfine all purpose flour
- 1 Pinch of fine sea salt
- 2 Teaspoon of baking powder
- ¼ Teaspoon of xanthan gum
- 1/3 Cup of unsweetened cocoa powder
- 1 Cup of unsweetened vanilla milk

DIRECTIONS:

1. Preheat your air fryer to about 350° F
2. Grease a baking pan that fits your air fryer basket with butter
3. Mix your ingredients into a food processor and whisk it for 1 to 2 minutes
4. Pour the batter into your prepared and greased pan Cover the baking tray with an aluminium foil paper and put it in the basket of the air fryer
5. Close the lid of your air fryer; then set the timer to about 35 minutes and the temperature to 345°
6. When the timer beeps, turn off the air fryer and remove your coffee cake to cool for 10 minutes
7. Dust the cake with cocoa powder; then serve and enjoy your cake!

AIR FRIED RASPBERRY COBBLERS

Prep Time: 10 Minutes | Cooking Time: 15 Minutes | Servings: 4

INGREDIENTS:

- 2 Cups of raspberries, blackberries and blueberries

- 1 Cup of all purpose flour
- ½ Of tick melted butter
- ½ Teaspoon of agave syrup
- 1 Large egg
- ½ Cup of Splenda of sugar
- Aluminium foil

DIRECTIONS:

1. Preheat your air fryer to about 350° F
2. Put the raspberries, the blackberries and the blueberries in a greased baking tray that fits your air fryer basket
3. Combine altogether the rest of the flour, the vanilla, the agave syrup and the ½ portion of the Splenda or sugar
4. Add the egg, the melted butter and toss in the berries
5. Pour the batter into the greased baking pan and top with the sugar
6. Cover your baking tray with a foil
7. Put the basket of the air fryer and close the lid and set the timer to about 15 minutes and the temperature for about 350° F
8. When the timer beeps, remove the tray from the air fryer and let the berry cobbler rest for about 10 minutes
9. Serve and enjoy your delicious and nutritious dessert!

MACADAMIA BISCUITS

Prep Time: 10 Minutes | Cooking Time: 20 Minutes | Servings: 8

INGREDIENTS:

- ½ Cup of softened butter
- ½ Cup of packed brown sugar
- 1/3 Cup of granulated sugar
- 2 and ½ tablespoons of peanut butter
- 2 Teaspoons of vanilla extract
- 1 and ¾ cups of all-purpose flour
- 2 Teaspoons of cornstarch
- 1 Teaspoon of baking soda
- ¼ Teaspoon of salt
- ½ Cup of roughly-chopped macadamia nuts
- ½ Cup of white chocolate chips
- 1 Pinch of Flaky sea salt

DIRECTIONS:

1. Preheat your air fryer to about 350° F
2. In a food processor; blend together the softened butter with the sugar on a medium speed for about 2 minutes.
3. Add the egg and the vanilla; then mix very well until it is very – well combined.
4. Sift in the flour, the cornstarch, the baking soda and the salt; whisk the ingredients on a low speed for about 2 minutes
5. Add the chocolate chips and the macadamia nuts until it is very-well combined
6. Scoop your obtained dough into the shape of balls
7. Line a baking tray with a parchment paper and line your balls in it
8. Sprinkle a little bit of salt on top of your biscuits; then put the tray in the basket of the air fryer and close the lid
9. Set the timer to about 17 minutes and the temperature to about 350° F
10. When the timer beeps, remove the biscuits from the air fryer and set it aside to cool for about 10 minutes
11. Serve and enjoy your salty biscuits!

COCOA AND VANILLA CUPCAKES

Prep Time: 10 Minutes | Cooking Time: 20 Minutes | Servings: 6

INGREDIENTS

- 1 Cup of unsweetened plain soy milk
- 1 Teaspoon of apple cider vinegar
- ¾ Cup of granulated sugar

- 1/3 Cup of vegetable oil
- 1 Teaspoon of pure vanilla extract
- ½ Teaspoon of vanilla extract
- 1 Cup of all-purpose flour
- 1/3 Cup of cocoa powder
- ¾ Teaspoon of baking soda
- ½ Teaspoon of baking powder
- ¼ Teaspoon of fine sea salt

DIRECTIONS

1. In a large bowl; mix altogether the vinegar with the soy milk and set the mixture aside for about 5 minutes
2. Add the oil, the sugar and the vanilla extract; then whisk very well until your ingredients become fluffy
3. In a separate bowl, mix the flour with the cocoa powder, the baking soda, the baking powder, and the salt.
4. Gradually add the dry ingredients to your wet ingredients and keep whisking for 1 minute
5. Preheat your air fryer to about 350°F; then line a muffin tin with foil liners
6. Pour the obtained batter into your prepared liners; make sure to fill about the ¾ of the muffin tins.
7. Put the baking pan in the air fryer basket and close the lid
8. Set the timer to about 20 minutes and the temperature to 345° F
9. When the timer beeps, remove the tray from the air fryer and transfer it to a wire rack to cool
10. Serve and enjoy your delicious dessert!

AIR FRIED CHOCOLATE RAMEKINS

Prep Time: 10 Minutes| Cooking Time: 10 Minutes | Servings: 4

INGREDIENTS

- 2 Tablespoons of self Raising Flour
- 4 Tablespoons of Caster Sugar
- 1 Cup of Dark Chocolate
- 1 Cup of butter
- 1 Orange; both the rind and the juice
- 2 Large eggs

DIRECTIONS:

1. Preheat your air fryer to about 360° F
2. Grease 4 steel or heat proof ramekins.
3. Start by melting the chocolate and the butter into a heat proof pan filled with water over a medium-high heat
4. In a small bowl, crack the eggs and beat with it the sugar
5. Remove the chocolate from the heat and add to it the mixture of the sugar and the eggs; then whisk very well.
6. Add the flour and mix the ingredients very well; then fill the ramekins, each with about 2/3 full with the mixture; then line the ramekins in the basket of the air fryer and close the lid
7. Set the timer to about 11 minutes and the temperature to 350°F
8. When the timer beeps, remove the ramekins from the air fryer and set it aside to cool for about 10 minutes; then put it over a serving dish and poke your fondant with a knife in the middle
9. Serve and enjoy with caramel sauce!

AIR FRIED ORANGE CAKE

Prep Time: 10 Minutes| Cooking Time: 30 Minutes | Servings: 4

INGREDIENTS:

- 3 Quartered oranges
- 6 Large eggs
- 2 cups of all purpose flour
- 1 Teaspoon of baking powder

- 3 Tablespoons of granulated maple syrup
- 1 Teaspoon of vanilla
- ¼ Teaspoon of salt

DIRECTIONS:

1. Start by putting the oranges into a large saucepan and add to it about ½ cup of water
2. Let the ingredients simmer into the water over a medium-low heat for about 30 minutes
3. Remove the oranges from the saucepan; then set it aside to cool
4. Preheat your air fryer to about 375° F
5. Grease a spring baking tray with a little bit of butter; then sprinkle a little bit of flour
6. Cut the oranges and blend the pieces with eggs into a blender
7. In a deep and large bowl, combine the almonds with the sugar and the baking powder; then mix very well
8. Add the flour and the orange mixture; then whisk very well
9. Pour the batter into the baking tray and put it in the basket of the air fryer; then close the lid and set the timer to about 25 to 30 minutes and the temperature to about 350° F
10. When the timer beeps, remove the cake from the air fryer and set it aside to cool for 5 minutes; then serve and enjoy it!

AIR FRIED GLAZED DONUT

Prep Time: 15 Minutes| Cooking Time: 25Minutes | Servings: 4

INGREDIENTS:

To make the donuts:
- 2 Tablespoons of softened butter
- ¼ Cup of sour cream
- 2 tbsp Trim Healthy Mama Gentle Sweet (or my combo of xylitol, erythritol, and stevia)
- ¼ Cup of flour
- ¼ Cup of all purpose flour+ ground flax
- 1 Large egg
- 1 Teaspoon of vanilla
- ½ Teaspoon of baking powder
- 1 Pinch of salt

For the topping of crumb:
- ½ Cup of flour
- 2 Teaspoon of all purpose flour
- 3 Tablespoon of softened butter
- 3 Tablespoons of sweetener

To make the glaze:
- 2 Tablespoons of butter
- ½ Cup of sweetener

DIRECTIONS:

1. Preheat your air fryer to about 350°F
2. In a large bowl; combine your ingredient altogether to form a batter; then grease a muffin tin with cooking spray
3. Divide your batter between the muffin holes; meanwhile, combine the ingredients of the crumbs in a bowl and mix it very well
4. Spread the crumbs with your hands over your already prepared donut batter
5. Put the baking tray in the basket of your air fryer and close the lid
6. Set the timer for 20 minutes and the temperature to about 365° F; in the meantime; prepare your glaze in a medium saucepan
7. Melt your butter in the saucepan and add the sweetener to it; then let cook on a low heat for about 10 minutes
8. When the timer beeps, remove the muffin tin from the Air fryer and set it aside to cool for about 5 minutes over a wire rack
9. Pour the glaze over your donuts; then repeat the same process until you finish all the donuts
10. Set the ingredients aside for the glaze to thicken for about 5 minutes
11. Serve and enjoy!

AIR FRIED BROWNIES

Prep Time: 10 Minutes | Cooking Time: 20 Minutes | Servings: 6

INGREDIENTS

- 2 Cups of all purpose flour
- 1 tbsp of arrowroot powder
- ½ tsp of baking soda
- ¼ tsp of salt
- 2 Large eggs
- 2 and ½ tbsp of lemon juice
- 1 tbsp of lemon zest
- 4 tbsp of raw honey
- ¼ Cup of vegetable oil
- ⅓ Cup of milk
- 2 tbsp of butter
- 1 tsp of vanilla extract

To make the glaze:

- 2 tbsp of milk
- 2 and ½ tsp of butter
- ½ tbsp of lemon juice
- 2 tsp of lemon zest
- 2 tsp of arrowroot powder
- 1 tsp of raw honey

DIRECTIONS

1. Mix the arrowroot powder, the all purpose flour, the baking soda and the salt in a large bowl
2. Whisk the eggs in another bowl with the lemon juice, the lemon zest, the honey, the oil, the milk, the butter and the vanilla extract
3. Add the dry ingredients to your wet ingredients and mix very well with a spatula
4. Line your Air Fryer pan with a parchment paper
5. Spread the batter over the pan and place the pan in your Air Fryer
6. Lock the lid of your Air Fryer and set the timer to about 20 minutes and the temperature to about 350° F
7. When the timer beeps; turn off your Air Fryer; then set the pan aside to cool for 10 minutes
8. In the meantime, prepare the glaze by mixing the ingredients in a bowl
9. Spread the glaze over your brownie
10. Cut the brownie into squares
11. Serve and enjoy your dessert!

AIR FRIED COCOA CAKE

Prep Time: 10 Minutes | Cooking Time: 20 Minutes | Servings: 2

INGREDIENTS

- 2 tbsp of organic unsweetened cocoa powder
- 2 tbsp of Erythritol
- 1 Pastured egg
- 1 tbsp of heavy cream
- ½ tsp of vanilla extract
- ¼ tsp of baking powder
- 1 tsp of salted butter
- 1 tbsp of butter

DIRECTIONS:

1. Combine the cocoa powder with the sweetener and the baking powder in a large bowl
2. Whisk your ingredients very well until it becomes mashed
3. In a second bowl; combine the egg with the heavy cream and the vanilla extract and whisk very well to combine
4. Mix your wet ingredients with your dry ingredients and combine until your ingredients become very well incorporated
5. Melt the butter in a small small bowl

6. Butter a heat proof ramekin with butter
7. Pour the obtained mixture into the ramekin and place the ramekin your Air Fryer basket
8. Lock the lid of your Air Fryer and set the timer to 3 minutes and the temperature to 350° F
9. When the timer beeps; turn off your Air Fryer
10. Soften the butter; then pour it over the cake
11. Serve and enjoy your delicious dessert!

AIR FRIED BERRY BROWNIES

Prep Time: 8 Minutes| Cooking Time: 20 Minutes | Servings: 4

INGREDIENTS

- 1 and ½ cups of softened butter
- 4 tbsp of granulated stevia
- ½ Cup of unsweetened cocoa powder
- 2 Medium eggs
- 1 tsp of vanilla
- 1 Cup of unsweetened shredded coconut
- 1 Cup of all purpose flour
- ½ tsp of baking powder
- 1 Cup of berries

DIRECTIONS:

1. Combine the butter and the sweetener and whisk until it becomes pale
2. Add the rest of the remaining ingredients except for the berries
3. Add the berries; then pour it over the brownie mixture
4. Spray your Air Fryer pan with cooking spray; then pour the mixture of the brownie in the baking pan
5. Place the pan in your Air Fryer and lock the lid
6. Set the timer for about 20 minutes and set the temperature for about 180°C/ 355° F
7. When the timer beeps; turn off your Air Fryer
8. Slice the brownies into squares; then serve and enjoy your dessert!

AIR FRIED CHOCOLATE FUDGES

Prep Time: 10 Minutes| Cooking Time: 20 Minutes | Servings: 4

INGREDIENTS

- 2 tbsp of cocoa powder
- ¼ Cup of egg whites
- 1 tbsp of vegetable oil
- 1 ½ cups o all purpose flour
- 2 tbsp chocolate chips

DIRECTIONS:

1. Preheat your Air Fryer to a temperature of about 185°C/ 375°F.
2. Combine all your ingredients except for the chocolate chips in a mixing bowl
3. Pour the mixture in a steel ramekin or a heat proof ramekin
4. Top the ramekin with the chocolate chips
5. Put the ramekin in your Air Fryer basket and lock the lid
6. Set the temperature to about 375° F and set the timer to about 20 minutes
7. When the timer beeps; turn off your Air Fryer and set the ramekin aside to cool for 5 minutes
8. Serve and enjoy your delicious dessert!

AIR FRIED CUSTARD

Prep Time: 8 Minutes| Cooking Time: 30 Minutes | Servings: 3

INGREDIENTS:

- 1 Cup of milk
- 4 Eggs
- 1/3 Cup of heavy cream
- 1/3 Cup of macadamia nut butter
- 1/3 Cup of erythritol
- 1 tsp of liquid Stevia
- 1 tsp of vanilla extract

DIRECTIONS:

1. Preheat your Air Fryer to 170° C/340° F
2. Add the milk to a medium bowl; then add the heavy cream
3. Add the vanilla extract; then add the 4 eggs and whisk very well
4. Add the sweeteners and the macadamia nut butter.
5. Keep stirring until your ingredients are very well combined
6. Fill your Air Fryer with about 1 inch of water
7. Place the ramekins in your Air Fryer pan and make sure they covered by about 1 inch of water
8. Fill your ramekins with the mixture of custard mixture.
9. Put the baking pan with the ramekins in your Air Fryer and lock the lid
10. Set the timer for about 30 minutes and set the temperature to about 345° F
11. When the timer beeps, turn off your Air Fryer and remove the pan from the Air Fryer
12. Set the ramekins aside to cool for about 20 minutes
13. Discard the ramekins from the Air Fryer pan and let it dry
14. Serve and enjoy your custard!

AIR FRIED BLUEBERRY SQUARES

Prep Time: 10 Minutes| Cooking Time: 20 Minutes | Servings: 6

INGREDIENTS

- 2 Cups of all purpose flour
- 1/3 Cup of Swerve Sweetener
- 1 tbsp of baking powder
- ¼ tsp of salt
- 2 Eggs
- ¼ Cup of heavy whipping cream
- ½ tsp of vanilla extract
- ¾ Cup of fresh blueberries

DIRECTIONS:

1. Preheat your Air Fryer to a temperature of about 325° F and line your Air Fryer pan with a parchment paper
2. Mix the flour with the sweetener, the all purpose flour, the baking powder and the salt in a large bowl
3. Add in the eggs; the whipping cream and the vanilla; then mix until your dough starts coming together
4. Add in the blueberries and gently whisk
5. Pat your dough into the Air Fryer pan lined with the baking sheet
6. Cut the dough into squares in a diagonal way; then cut each square into two triangles
7. Place the pan in the Air Fryer and lock the lid
8. Set the timer to about 20 minutes and set the temperature to 170° c/ 340° F
9. When the timer beeps, turn off your Air Fryer; then let the cones cool for about 5 minutes
10. Serve and enjoy your scones!

AIR FRIED CINNAMON CAKE

Prep Time: 12 Minutes| Cooking Time: 20 Minutes | Servings: 4

INGREDIENTS:

To make the base

- Separated large eggs
- 6 Ounces of cream cheese
- ¼ Cup of erythritol
- ¼ tsp of liquid Stevia
- 2 tsp of vanilla extract
- ¼ tsp of cream of tartar

To make the filling

- 1 and ½ cups of all purpose flour
- 1 tbsp of cinnamon
- ¼ Cup of butter
- ¼ Cup of maple syrup
- ¼ Cup of erythritol

DIRECTIONS:

1. Preheat your Air Fryer to a temperature of about oven to 325°F. If you're using a glass baking dish, use 300°F.
2. Separate the whites of the eggs from the yolks; then cream the egg yolks with about ¼ cup of the Erythritol and about ¼ tsp of the stevia liquid
3. Add the cream cheese; then combine very well until you form a tick mixture
4. Beat the egg whites with the cream of tartar and mix until the stiff peak starts forming
5. Add the egg whites to the mixture of the egg yolk and whisk
6. Grease your Air Fryer pan with cooking spray; then pour the batter in the baking pan
7. Prepare the filling by mixing 1 and ½ cups of flour, 1 tbsp of cinnamon, the ½ stick of butter, the ¼ cup of maple syrup; and the ¼ cup of Erythritol
8. Combine your ingredients very well; then just add the mixture to the top of the Air Fryer pan without mixing
9. Lock the lid of your Air Fryer and set the timer to about 15 to 18 minutes and set the temperature to about 180° C/360° F
10. When the timer beeps, turn off your Air Fryer; then remove the pan and let it cool for about 10 minutes
11. Slice your cake; then serve and enjoy it!

AIR FRIED NUT CLUSTERS

Prep Time: 10 Minutes | Cooking Time: 15 Minutes | Servings: 5

INGREDIENTS:

- 1 Cup of erythritol
- 1 Pound of pecan halves
- 1 Large egg white
- 1 tbsp of water
- 2 tsp of ground cinnamon
- 2 tsp of ground nutmeg
- 1 tsp of salt
- 1 tbsp cooking spray
- 1 tsp of pumpkin pie spice

DIRECTIONS:

1. Preheat your Air Fryer to a temperature of about 350° F
2. Mix your dry ingredients together; then whisk the egg white with 1 tbsp of water
3. Whisk your ingredients until it becomes fluffy
4. Add the pecans to the egg white mixture; then add in the pecans
5. Add the pecans to your dry ingredients and stir
6. Spray your Air Fryer pan with cooking spray and line it with a baking sheet
7. Pour the pecans in the baking pan into an even layer; then place the pan in the Air Fryer and lock the lid
8. Set the timer to about 15 minutes and the temperature to 345° F
9. When the timer beeps; turn off your Air Fryer; then set the pecans aside to cool for 10 minutes
10. Serve and enjoy your pecan clusters.

AIR FRIED HONEY COOKIES

Prep Time: 10 Minutes | Cooking Time: 15 Minutes | Servings: 6

INGREDIENTS

- 1 Cup of Butter
- ½ cup of raw honey
- 2 Cups of all purpose flour
- ½ Cup of chocolate chips
- 1 Tbsp of milk

DIRECTIONS:

1. Preheat your Air Fryer to a temperature of about 180° C/360° F
2. Beat the honey with the butter in a bowl; then add the flour and mix very well
3. Smash the chocolate with a rolling pin; then add the chocolate chunks to your bowl
4. Gradually add the milk and mix your ingredients very well
5. Line your Air Fryer baking pan with a baking sheet; then spoon the cookies in the pan
6. Spoon the cookies over the baking sheet; then place the pan in the Air Fryer and lock the lid
7. Set the timer to about 8 minutes and the temperature to about 350° F
8. Remove the cookies from your Air Fryer

AIR FRIED MACAROONS

Prep Time: 10 Minutes | Cooking Time: 15 Minutes | Servings: 4

INGREDIENTS

To make the shells:
- 2 Egg white large egg whites
- ½ Oz of erythritol
- 3 oz of blanched almonds
- ½ Teaspoons of matcha tea powder
- 5 Oz of powdered erythritol

To make the topping of the pistachios
- 1 and ½ oz of unsalted pistachios
- 1/8 Teaspoon of stevia extract
- ½ Teaspoon of vanilla extract
- 2/3 oz of unsalted butter

Directions

1. Start by making the shells
2. Preheat your air fryer to about 325° F and lien a baking sheet with a parchment paper
3. Ground the toasted almonds; then pulse it with a food processor for about 40 seconds
4. Add the erythritol and keep processing until you obtain fine all purpose flour by processing for 1 additional minute and with a processor,
5. Beat in the eggs and mix all of the ingredients together until you get a fluffy mixture
6. Add the powder of matcha and when the batter gets a green color; add the about 1/3 of your mixture of erythritol with the all purpose flour and mix on a very low speed
7. With a spatula, add mix your ingredients very well; then stir in the rest of the erythritol mixture; then transfer your mixture very well to a plastic bag for pastry; then cut the tip into a hole of ½ inch; then start piping the cookies on the baking pan lined with the parchment paper
8. Set the cookies aside to dry for about 50 minutes
9. Put the baking tray in the air fryer basket and close the lid
10. Set the timer to about 15 minutes and the temperature to about 325° F
11. When the timer beeps, remove the cookies from the air fryer and set it aside to cool for 10 minute: meanwhile prepare the pistachio topping by grounding the pistachio with the erythritol.
12. With an electric mixer, combine the butter with the stevia very well; then add the pistachio mixture and add the extract of the vanilla
13. Line your pistachio macaroons on a serving platter and fill each with a spoon of the cream of the pistachio; then cover the shell with another shell with a similar size.
14. Set the macaroons in the refrigerator for about 30 minutes; then serve and enjoy!

Cooking Conversion Charts:

Volume (liquid)

Metric	US Customary
6.1 ml	1/8 teaspoon
2.51 ml	1/2 teaspoon
5.1 ml	1 teaspoon
15.2 ml	1 tablespoon
118.13 ml	1/2 cup
238 ml	1 cup or 8 fluid ounces
472 ml	2 cups or 1 pint
945 ml	4 cups or 1 quart
1.8 liters	8 cups or 1/2 gallon
3.9 liters	1 gallon

Equivalents of Volume (liquid)*

3.5 teaspoons	1.5 tablespoon	0.8 fluid ounce
2 ¼ tablespoons	1/8 cup	1.1 fluid ounce
4 ¼ tablespoons	½ cup	2.1 fluid ounces
5 ¼ tablespoons	1/3 cup	2.8 fluid ounces
15.8 tablespoons	1 ¼ cups	8.1 fluid ounces
2 ¼ cups	1 ¼ pint	16.3 fluid ounces
2 ¼ pints	1 ¼ quart	32.2 fluid ounces
4 ¼ quarts	1 ¼ gallon	128.1 fluid ounces

Oven Temperatures in US

US contemporary	Metric
251° F	122° C
301° F	148° C
351° F	176° C
401° F	205° C
452° F	231° C

(mass) Weight

US contemporary (in ounces)	Metric (in grams)
1/2 ounce	13.9 grams
1.2 ounce	28.1 grams
3.1 ounces	85.2 grams
3.5 ounces	100.1 grams
4.1 ounces	114 grams
8.2 ounces	226 grams
12.1 ounces	341 grams

Alphabetical Index:

A

Acorn Squash 38

Air Fried Grit Patties Breakfast 19

Air Fryer Greek Style Beef Chops 64

Air Fryer Macadamia And Rosemary Crusted Lamb 68

Apple Chips 34

Asian-Style Vegetable Spring Rolls 39

Asparagus 33

Aspragus Salad 44

Avocado 30

B

Bacon And Sweet Potato Salad 44

Bacon And Sweet Potato Salad 46

Beef And Salad 61

Beef Burgers 64

Beef Fajitas 62

Beef Liver 67

Beef Meatballs 61

Beef Meatloaf 60

Beef Mignon With Herbs 63

Beef Rellenos 60

Beef Satay 66

Beef Teriyaki 63

Beef With Herbs 62

Beef With Veggies 65

Beet And Carrots Veggie Salad 43

Bell Pepper Salad 43

Berry Brownies 100

Blueberry Squares 101

Breadsticks 37

Breakfast Egg Muffins 20

Breakfast Hash browns 23

Broccoli Florets With Sesame Seeds 30

Broccoli Fritters 29

Brown Bread 89

Brownies 99

Brussels Sprouts 27

Buffalo Chicken With Blue Cheese 52

Burrito Chicken 50

Butter Bread 91

C

Caesar Salad 47

Carrots 38

Cashews With Paprika 41

Cauliflower Bake 84

Cheddar Chicken Muffins 51

Cheese Bread 93

Cheese Chicken Wings 49

Cheese Sticks 32

Chicken And Sweet Potato 58

Chicken And Sweet Potatoes 59

Chicken Bake 57

Chicken Bites 53

Chicken Breasts 48

Chicken Chops With Cashews 51

Chicken Nuggets With Mayonnaise 49

Chicken Spinach Nest 53

Chicken Stuffed Macaroni With Cashews 56

Chicken Thighs 54

Chicken Wings 54

Chicken With Broccoli 52

Chickpeas 39

Chinese Style Chicken 55

Chocolate Bars 94

Chocolate Fudges 100

Chocolate Muffins 95

Chocolate Ramekins 97

Cinnamon Cake 101

Cloud Pancakes 26

Cocoa And Vanilla Cupcakes 96

Cocoa Cake 99

Coconut And Cheddar Cheese Shrimp 81

Corn On The Cob With Lobsters 83

Crispy Chicken 57

Crispy Feta Cheese Fries 28

Crispy Tofu With Cornstarch Salad 42

Crispy Vanilla Bread 87

Crusted Lamb With Orange 69

Curried Prawns 82

Custard 100

E

Egg And Avocado Salad 45

Egg Rolls 21

Eggplant Fritters 86

Eggplants With Zaatar 27

Eggs In Avocado 25

F

Farro Salad 41

Fish And Chips 81

Fish Fillets 79

Fish Nuggets 79

Fish Tacos 82

Flan 94

Flat Breakfast Bread 24

Fluffy Breakfast Donuts 19

Foccacia Bread With Olives 91

French Toast With Blueberries 20

Frozen Shrimp 81

G

Garlic Bagels 92

Garlic Bread 89

Glazed Donut 98

Granola Breakfast 22

Green Beans 34

H

Halibut With Nuts 78

Honey Cookies 103

I

Italian Pork 75

J

Jalapeno Wraps With Bacon 37

K

Kale Chips 35

Kale Nuggets 85

L

Lamb Burgers 69

Lamb Chops With Herbs 71

Lamb Koftas 71

Lamb Ribs 70

M

Macadamia Biscuits 96

Macaroons 103

Mongolian Beef 65

Mushroom Frittata 22

Mushrooms 29

Mushrooms With Teriyaki Sauce 40

Mustard Crusted Pork 74

N

Nut Clusters 102

O

Onion 32

Orange Almond Bread 90

Orange Cake 97

P

Pancakes 26

Paprika Chicken 50

Pear Salad 45

Pecan Oat Breakfast 23

Pizza 38

Pork 76

Pork Chops With Sweet Potatoes 76

Pork Sausage 72

Pork Shoulder 77

Pork Tenderloin With Paprika 73

Pork With Cheese 72

Pork With Sake 77

Pork With Vegetables 74

Pork With Zucchini 75

Potato Bake 36

Potato Buns 39

Potato Chips 31

Potato Fritters 40

Potato Skins 28

Potatoes 29

Potatoes And Beets 40

Potatoes And Parsnips Salad 46

Pumpkin And Cinnamon Swirl Bread 88

Q

Quick Bread 90

R

Radish 33

Raspberry Cobblers 95

Rosemary Bread 89

S

Salmon With Panko Breadcrumbs 80

Salmon With Soy Sauce 79

Sausage Breakfast 24

Scallops 82

Seed bread 88

Sesame Buns 92

Shrimp With Oregano 78

Spare Ribs 66

Spicy Steak With Mushrooms 66

Spicy Bagels 93

Spicy Beef Steak 63

Spicy Lamb 68

Spinach Stuffed Chicken 58

Squid Rings 83

Steak With Pesto 67

Stuffed Avocado 31

Stuffed Chicken 55

Stuffed Flat Bread With Lamb 70

Stuffed Jumbo Shells 56

Stuffed Mushrooms 31

Stuffed Pork Chops With Cheese And Kale 72

T

Tandoori Chicken 48

Teriyaki Pork Ribs 73

Tilapia 80

Tofu And Lettuce Salad 42

Tomato With Herbs 84

Tomatoes 35

Turkey Tenders 48

V

Vanilla Cake 95

Vegetables 36

Vegetables Salad 43

Veggies With Olive And Coriander 86

W

Walnut Bread 87

Whole Chicken 51

Whole Meal Cinnamon Toast 21

Whole Wheat Almond Bread 87

Whole Wheat Banana Toast 25

Wrapped Halloumi Cheese With Bacon 34

Z

Zucchini Patties With Cashew Cheese 85

Printed in Great Britain
by Amazon